INNOVATION TRAINING

Ruth Ann Hattori
Joyce Wycoff

Exercises, Handouts, Assessments, and Tools to Help You:

- Understand the Principles and Practices of Innovation
- Build Competencies and Drive Innovation Throughout Your Organization
- Become a More Effective and Efficient Facilitator
- Ensure Training Is on Target and Gets Results

ASTD
WORKPLACE LEARNING & PERFORMANCE
PRESS

Alexandria, VA

ASTD Press is an internationally renowned source of insightful and practical information on workplace learning and performance topics, including training basics, evaluation and return-on-investment (ROI), instructional systems development (ISD), e-learning, leadership, and career development.

Ordering information: Books published by ASTD Press can be purchased by visiting our website at store.astd.org or by calling 800.628.2783 or 703.683.8100.

Terms of Use for accompanying CD-ROM material with ASTD Press Titles: As the purchaser, you can modify or otherwise customize the slides and other materials in the purchased book by opening and editing them in the appropriate application. However, all uses must denote the original source of the material—presenting this content as your own work is a breach of copyright law. You may indicate that a document was adapted from the purchased book and copyrighted by ASTD. The proper form for this identification is:

"Adapted from materials found in *Innovation Training* published by the American Society for Training & Development (ASTD), 2004. All rights reserved."

Library of Congress Control Number: 2004101571

ISBN-10: 1-56286-366-5
ISBN-13: 978-1-56286-366-1

Acquisitions and Development Editor: Mark Morrow
Copyeditor: Christine Cotting, UpperCase Publication Services, Ltd.
Interior Design and Production: UpperCase Publication Services, Ltd.
Cover Design: Ana Ilieva
Cover Illustration: Todd Davidson

The ASTD Trainer's WorkShop Series is designed to be a practical, hands-on road map to help you quickly develop training in key business areas. Each book in the series offers all the exercises, handouts, assessments, structured experiences, and ready-to-use presentations needed to develop effective training sessions. In addition to easy-to-use icons, each book in the series includes a companion CD-ROM with PowerPoint presentations and electronic copies of all supporting material featured in the book.

Other books in the Trainer's WorkShop Series:

- *New Supervisor Training*
  John E. Jones and Chris W. Chen

- *Customer Service Training*
  Maxine Kamin

- *New Employee Orientation Training*
  Karen Lawson

- *Leading Change Training*
  Jeffrey Russell and Linda Russell

- *Leadership Training*
  Lou Russell

- *Coaching Training*
  Chris W. Chen

- *Project Management Training*
  Bill Shackelford

Contents

Innovation is as much a mindset as it is a set of principles, practices, skills, tools, and techniques. It is a belief in the future; conviction that things can always be better; confidence in the positive force of new ideas; faith in the power of people working together toward a common objective; trust in imagination, ingenuity, intuition, and instincts as well as rational thought, analysis, evaluation, and measurement. Although it is almost impossible to train a mindset, through training using novel skills, tools, and techniques and then seeing previously unimagined results, a new mindset gradually emerges.

As leaders and training professionals, you have great influence in facilitating development of the innovation mindset and the future success of your organization. In our hypercompetitive world, the ability to develop novel and better products, processes, services, and delivery mechanisms that create new and added value is critical to an organization's viability. Leaders, from Tom Peters to Peter Drucker, have emphasized the importance of innovation, condensing it to the catch phrase "Innovate or Die!"

It is our hope that this book will make your learning journey easier by providing you with the tools you need to champion innovation and launch innovation training in your organization. *Innovation Training* is about developing new competencies for innovation—competencies that can be spread across your entire organization as you help your co-workers make innovation part of their jobs. With the information contained in this book you can become a leader of innovation, a strategic partner in creating the future of your organization.

The innovation framework and learning tools presented here were created over the past decade's work with the InnovationNetwork and the Innovation-University (IU), and with many clients. InnovationNetwork was formed in

1993 as a way to share information among people working in the area of innovation. Through this network we sponsored annual conferences bringing together people from all over the world to share tools, techniques, experiences, and ideas about how to make innovation an organization-wide competency.

As we started this journey in the early 1990s, talking to people from corporations large and small and from nonprofit and government organizations, we realized that innovation was approximately where "quality" was in the early 1980s. People were talking about it, but the discipline of the field, the frameworks, tools, and techniques hadn't been developed. We formed Innovation-University in 1995 as a way to begin to develop and codify the discipline. IU students met quarterly with faculty members to tour and learn from some of the leading organizations in the United States, Canada, and Peru. Students had an opportunity to see, hear, and touch innovation in action at places such as 3M, IDEO Product Design, Cirque du Soleil, Nortel, Dell Computer, GSD&M Advertising, the Smithsonian Institution, NASA, Celestial Seasonings, and Best Buy. Out of these meetings grew a deeper understanding of the "system" of innovation and a desire for a framework to help people grasp the complexity of innovation.

Early IU students were challenged to develop a framework for innovation as part of their project-based action learning program. Over time, as they searched for a metaphor to use as the basis of the framework, they eliminated many static models, such as pyramids and Venn diagrams, and finally settled on an organic metaphor to capture the growing, shifting, living properties of innovation. This framework known as the InnovationDNA™, has been used by organizations around the world and been revised several times before it reached the form you will see in this book and on the accompanying CD.

We are delighted to be part of this training series, which offers you not only a practical, hands-on compendium of training tools, techniques, workshop design guides, and checklists but also a CD that includes PowerPoint slides, handouts, and exercises to print and copy. The American Society for Training & Development is truly modeling innovation as it finds new ways to create value by getting "out of the book" with this series.

Innovation is a journey that seems to attract the most wonderful people, full of curiosity, optimism, and a belief in the power of people working together to create new possibilities. Welcome to the journey! We hope this book serves you well, and we invite you to explore the InnovationNetwork Website, www.thinksmart.com, which is a treasure trove of information, case studies, and other materials useful to innovation leaders.

We wish you great joy and success with your efforts to stimulate innovation within your organization. And we wish you fun—an official *innovation value* that always seems to show up when innovation is really cooking. So we encourage you to have fun and find ways to design fun into all of your training sessions.

Ruth Ann Hattori and Joyce Wycoff

June 2004

Acknowledgments

◆

Writing a book is never just the work of the authors—there are a thousand shoulders we are standing on and naming any risks overlooking many. But there are some people who have to be acknowledged for their incredible help and support.

Special thanks to Mark Morrow, our editor, who breathed life into this project and gave us the opportunity to pull years' worth of work together into a format that can be easily used by trainers and facilitators in organizations large and small. Our deep appreciation goes to Christine Cotting who "test drove" a complicated format to make sure all the words made sense and the numbered handouts and attachments were consistent. We take full responsibility for any errors that may have slipped past her eagle eye.

We also want to thank all the people who have learned with us through the years and cheerfully let us try out new ideas, theories, and activities—especially Dana Wolcott, Jerry McNellis, Deanna Berg, Charlie Prather, Debra Giampoli, Allen Fahden, Virginia Albanese, Andrea Woodward, David Neenan, Marsha McArthur, Allen Liff, Cynthia Carlisle, Suzanne Merritt, Anne Blouin, Robert Tucker, Tom Asacker, Anne Robinson, Jonathan Vehar, Gerald Haman, Alex Pattakos, Tom Drucker, Alain Rostain, Marian Their, Lynne Snead, Russ Ward, and Christopher Goodrich. And, in loving memory of Layne Cannon, our steadfast mentor.

Why Innovation?

- ◆ Explanation of why innovation matters
- ◆ Discussion of how training can build innovation
- ◆ Description of the three levels of Innovation Basics Training
- ◆ How to use this book and the accompanying CD

Think about pushing an empty shopping cart down a road. In front of you the road branches and you have a choice to go right or left. This is an image we use often in our workshops and keynote addresses. The empty shopping cart is a metaphor for an organization's relentless pursuit of increased revenues, reduced costs, improved customer satisfaction and ways to get to market faster, safer, and more effectively. This metaphor also works in our own lives as we look for ways to enhance our homes, our relationships, and our physical and emotional well-being and that of our family, friends, neighbors, and communities.

In this image we're on a path that is quickly approaching a critical juncture. Do we go right or left? The problem is that neither path looks like it leads to a supermarket or other place to fill our carts. And, that brings us to innovation, that search for a new way, a better answer, a previously unseen possibility.

In and of itself innovation is a complex system that encompasses everything about an organization—the people, infrastructure, and culture; the practices and processes; and of course the outcomes and fruits of its efforts. In this book we're going to focus on organizational innovation and the principles of innovation that will lay groundwork for you to help your organization find its unique path to a bright future of unlimited possibilities.

How This Book and CD Can Help You

This book and the accompanying CD are intended to be a *work*book. It will guide you to an understanding of the principles and practices of innovation. It will help you develop training programs that will enhance the innovation competency of people within your organization. Although we will be providing specific tools, learning activities, and sample workshop agendas, we want to encourage you to make these materials your own. Adding your unique perspective, examples, and stories to tailor the material to your specific audience will bring your sessions alive.

The Value of Innovation

Most companies know that innovation—*people implementing new ideas that create value*—is important, even imperative, to their futures. However, they often get so caught up in day-to-day operations and the quarterly return mindset that they put off actually doing what's needed to create the systems and competencies necessary to become truly innovative. Here are some recent statistics reported by Imaginatik Research on their Website, www.imaginatik.com:

- Innovative companies, defined by "percentage of revenue generated from products less than 5 years old," experience *profit growth at four times the rate of non-innovative organizations (Business Horizons 1996,* emphasis added).

- Innovation is a critical issue for senior executives. A 1998 Watson Wyatt survey of 400 companies found that 70 percent of companies' mission statements and top objectives mentioned innovation.

- But few companies have the processes and infrastructure in place to manage innovation. A survey of 350 organizations, conducted in 2000 by CBI and 3M Innovation, found that less than 15 percent of companies have any information technology (IT) systems in place to manage innovation, and only 40 percent have established any formal procedures.

These statistics portray a business climate of talking rather than doing, of not "walking the talk." So the question is no longer, "*Should* we be focused on innovation?" It is now a series of questions, including "*How* should we go about innovating? How *much* should we do? What is the *most effective* way to become more innovative? and "What should we do *first?*"

How Training Can Help Build Innovation

For too many years, innovation was considered something that either existed or didn't. You either had it or you didn't, and if you didn't, too bad. Although much of innovation is art, there is an equal measure of science and both are enhanced by a discipline, a way of approaching problems and opportunities with a rich toolkit that makes the apparent "magic" of innovation more predictable.

The curriculum presented here is for organizations interested in developing new possibilities through thinking and acting more creatively, collaborating more effectively, and implementing new ideas more rigorously. It is for all the people who have never thought of themselves as "creative" and for the folks who seem to come up with an idea a minute. It is for those totally new to innovation and for those looking to refresh their innovation toolbox. And, it's for all trainers who are seeking ways to unlock the ideas trapped behind the mental doors that workers often don't even know exist. This workbook offers a language and a framework that will help your entire organization learn how "innovation happens" and it provides an array of tools that can be used by people at every organizational level to make the principles of innovation operative.

Innovation Basics Training at Three Levels

The training programs offered in this book are focused on three separate entity levels: individual, group or team, and organization. As you begin to design your innovation training program, you may want to keep the following illustration in mind:

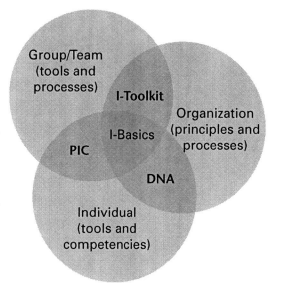

Innovation in organizations is generally a group activity done by individuals with varying degrees of innovation competence. Training at each of the three levels is important to the overall development of a sustainable innovation competency in your organization. However, each level has its own focus and purpose:

♦ **Organization:** At this level, you will be trying to build awareness of the overall principles and processes of innovation. The workshops at this level can be offered to anyone within the organization and are designed in easy-to-use one-hour segments that can be offered as brown-bag lunch workshops, as an ongoing series, or as parts of a more comprehensive half-day or full-day training format. These workshops are built around the InnovationDNA Framework of Principles (DNA).

◆ **Team/Group:** When people are ready to take on a specific innovation project they need specific tools and a process to help them be more effective and successful. The primary workshop to help teams is Creativity Made Simple, a half-day exploration that provides attendees with an array of powerful divergence and convergence tools.

◆ **Individual:** Developing personal understanding and competencies in innovation is an important part of the training process. The Personal Innovation Competency (PIC) half-day workshop focuses on this level and provides an overview of the most important competencies required for innovation.

How to Use This Workbook Most Effectively

You can use this book to prepare for your innovation training program in two ways:

1. **Predesigned workshops:** There are several model training sessions that incorporate tools into workshops of various lengths. They are designed so that they can be mixed and matched to fit your target audience and their particular needs. See the one-hour sessions in chapters 6 and 7 and the half-day sessions in chapters 8 and 9.

2. **Elements for design-your-own workshops:** You may also want to design your own sessions. Chapter 10 provides many learning activities handouts and PowerPoint presentations that can be used in various programmatic combinations. Use them as they are or add them to your own activities. See chapters 10 and 11 for these elements.

What's in This Workbook and on the CD?

All of the training materials in this workbook are also included on the accompanying CD so that you can easily run PowerPoint presentations and print out and copy other materials. To get a sense of your many options, review the contents of the CD to see how they relate to the items in the printed book. Read the document *How to Use the Contents of the CD.doc* included on the CD and read appendix A, "Using the Compact Disc," in the back of the workbook. Below is an overview of the materials included.

WORKSHOPS, LEARNING ACTIVITIES, HANDOUTS, AND SLIDE PRESENTATIONS

The workshops in chapters 6, 7, 8, and 9 incorporate learning activities, handouts, and PowerPoint slide presentations in various combinations. For easy reference we have grouped the activities in chapter 10, the handouts in chapter 11, and thumbnail versions of the slides in the chapters where they are discussed.

The learning activities in this workbook are designed to help participants acquire skills by using tools and techniques in near–real-world ways. In many cases you will be given an issue to focus on as you introduce new tools. At other times you will be guided to think of a unique issue of interest to your specific audience. Each activity includes the following elements:

- ◆ an abstract
- ◆ target audience
- ◆ goals and objectives
- ◆ materials list
- ◆ time
- ◆ instructions
- ◆ debriefing guidance (when appropriate)

Slides that accompany the activities are gathered into ready-made PowerPoint presentations and referenced appropriately. Full-color versions of the presentations as well as black-and-white versions that you can print as handouts or as projection masters are on the CD.

For each workshop in this book we have provided a map that gives you a bird's-eye view of the workshop, including timing, handouts, and learning activities. The full version of each map is only on the CD; a condensed black-and-white version of each workshop's map appears in chapters 6 through 9.

Icons

For your easy reference, icons have been included in the outside margins of this workbook pages. They will help you identify key items in a chapter or activity and easily locate specific materials. Here is what the icons look like and what they indicate:

CD: This icon indicates materials included on the CD accompanying this workbook.

Clock: This icon indicates suggested timeframes for an activity.

Handout: This icon indicates handouts you can print or copy and then use in ways that enhance the training experience.

Key Point: This icon will alert you to key points that should be emphasized in relation to a particular topic.

Learning Activity: This icon appears when an agenda includes a learning activity.

PowerPoint item: This icon indicates PowerPoint presentations and slides that can be used individually. These presentations and slides are on the CD included with your workbook, and copies of the slides appear within the relevant chapters. Instructions for using PowerPoint slides and the CD are included in the appendix.

Tool: This icon points out a reference to a training aid that can be printed in color and used to illustrate the topic being addressed.

What to Do Next: This icon denotes recommendations for what to do after completing a particular section.

What to Do Next

- ◆ Read the next chapter to learn about the theories that form the foundation for the activities and workshops included in this book.

- ◆ Talk to people in your organization about their approaches to innovation and how your culture supports (or blocks) creativity.

- ◆ Think about why innovation is important and how it can help your organization reach its objectives.

◆ ◆ ◆

The next chapter will introduce an overview of the innovation process and the InnovationDNA, a framework of principles that will help you understand the system of innovation. This is a key concept that will form the foundation of all the innovation workshops you conduct.

The Innovation Process

- Definition of innovation

- Introduction of the InnovationDNA Framework of Principles

- Discussion of how to change organization culture

There is no formula or quick fix for innovation. To be an innovative organization means being smart in a thousand different ways. Most organizations are already smart in many ways or they wouldn't still be in business. But organizations may be unconsciously competent. That is, they don't know or have not articulated what it is that makes them successful as innovators. The hazard is that because they don't know what's making them successful, they often create new strategies, policies, or procedures that undermine their success rather than enhance it.

One of the goals of training, and of this book, is to help organizations become more conscious of the underlying principles, practices, and skills that support innovation and organizational success. Innovation is not and should not be an isolated initiative in an organization. Innovation efforts should build on current strengths and strategies by identifying those areas where the organization could be even smarter.

The spectrum of innovation is vast. It ranges from incremental innovation—which can be small but important improvements to an existing product, service, or process—to breakthrough or disruptive innovations that cause entire industries or frames of reference to change. By definition, however, even incremental changes must produce added value in order to be called innovation.

The principles, processes, tools, and techniques introduced in this book and its training designs can be applied to the entire spectrum of innovation. The differences in outcomes, be they incremental or totally disruptive, are more linked to the initial purpose or charter of a given innovation project or initiative. You can bring value to any innovation effort of individuals and teams in your organization with the tools contained here.

InnovationDNA—A Framework of Principles

One of the first tasks facing anyone who wants to lead an innovation effort is to build a common understanding of the definition of innovation. The most common point of confusion is the distinction between creativity and innovation. The definition we have developed and tested with clients for the past several years is this:

Innovation is PEOPLE creating value by implementing new ideas.

There are four critical pieces of that definition:

1. **People**—innovation is done only by people, and generally only by groups of people working collaboratively. They may engage technology and other resources in the process of innovation, but only people can generate and implement new ideas that create value.

2. **Creating value**—the purpose of innovation is to create value—value for the customer (internal or external), for the organization, community, or other stakeholders.

3. **Implementing**—innovation is only finished when an idea has been put into action and there is a result that has created value, be that a new process, product, service, delivery mechanism, or system.

4. **New ideas**—innovation requires new ideas, new ways of looking at problems and opportunities. Ideas are gossamer pieces of fluff without value by themselves, but woven together with purpose and skill they become the stuff of legends.

To implement this definition, an organization needs to have an organizing structure to help guide the development of competency. The InnovationDNA is a framework of principles that provides this structure. At the highest level, there are three main parts of the framework: the operational principles, the organizational culture that forms the backdrop for making innovation "happen," and the context for innovation—the way we and our organizations operate in the world.

Take a look at the depiction of these parts in figure 2–1 and read on for more information about them (a color version of the graphic is on the CD, identified as Figure 2–2.pdf).

1. **Operational principles:** Innovation is sparked by new ideas; change; passion; shifts in trends, demographics, technologies; and world events. The operational principles of innovation are the DNA helix portion of the Innovation-DNA framework:

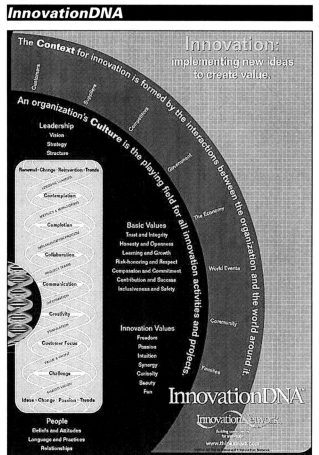

Figure 2–1
InnovationDNA

   ◆ **Challenge—the Pull.** Innovation, by definition, means doing things differently, exploring new territory, taking risks. There has to be a reason for rocking the boat and that's the vision of what could be...the challenge. The bigger the challenge and the commitment to it, the more energy the innovation efforts will focus on the issue at hand.

   ◆ **Customer Focus—the Push.** All innovation should be focused on creating value for the customer, whether that customer is internal or external. Interaction with customers and an understanding of their needs are two of the best stimulators of new possibilities and major motivators for implementing them.

   ◆ **Creativity—the Brain.** Everything starts from an idea and the best way to get a great high-potential concept is to generate a lot of ideas. Although creativity is a natural ability of every person, the skill of developing a lot of ideas and then crafting them into a working concept can be enhanced through training and exercise. A primary role of leadership is to provide direction and stimuli to spur creativity.

- **Communication—the Lifeblood.** Open communication of information, ideas, and feelings is the lifeblood of innovation. Both infrastructure and advocacy must exist in an organizational system to promote the free flow of information. Organizations that restrict this flow risk atrophy and even death.

- **Collaboration—the Heart.** Innovation is a group process. It feeds on interaction, information, and the power of teams. It is stifled by restrictive structures and policies as well as overly competitive environments and incentive systems that reward only individual efforts.

- **Completion—the Muscle.** Innovations are projects that are successfully realized through superior, defined processes and strong implementation skills—decision making, delegating, scheduling, monitoring, and receiving feedback from customers (internal or external) about the new concept. And when projects are completed (successfully or unsuccessfully) they should be celebrated.

- **Contemplation—the Ladder to Future Innovation.** Making objective assessments of the outcomes, benefits, and costs of new projects is essential. Gleaning the lessons learned from both fruitful and failed projects builds a wisdom base that creates an upward cycle of success. Documenting and evaluating projects is a critical step that helps perpetuate innovation.

2. **Culture:** Whereas the operational principles of the InnovationDNA depict *how* innovation happens in an organization, innovation results are highly dependent on the *who* of innovation—the people, relationships, and values that make up an organization's culture. Culture is the playing field for all innovation projects and activities. Although innovation is "for the sake of" creating value for customers or a lofty vision, the organizational culture must be fertile for the seeds of ideas and solutions to grow. A flexible environment that empowers people, welcomes ideas, tolerates risk, celebrates success, fosters synergy, and encourages fun is crucial. Creating such a climate

may also be the biggest challenge facing all organizations that want to be more innovative.

An innovative culture consists of four major components:

- **Leadership**—the role models who see the future possibilities. Strategies are put into place because leaders can envision a bright future and identify opportunities that can pave the path to success. Engaging the hearts of people and providing the necessary support are imperative to make the vision reality. We especially like the wisdom of the sixth-century B.C. Chinese philosopher, Lao Tzu who said:

  A leader is best when people barely know he exists, when his work is done, his aim fulfilled, they will say: we did it ourselves.

- **People—the Source of Innovation.** Nothing happens without people. Every organization has a "personality" that comes from its collective and shared beliefs, attitudes, and behaviors, and most of all from the relationships among its people.

- **Basic Values—the Backbone.** Basic values define an organization: trust and respect, learning, commitment, inclusiveness, and contribution are the kinds of principles that help an organization hold its shape in the frantic pace of global business. They provide the backbone for decisions and the foundation for shaping strategic alliances.

- **Innovation Values.** These form the mindset that makes the impossible possible. Beyond basic values, there are some drivers that can transform the mundane into the compelling and an ordinary project into a stellar new business. Freedom to explore new possibilities, intuition, curiosity, fun, and synergy are just a few of the ideals that create the "magic" in innovative organizations.

3. **Context:** There is also a *where* of innovation—the context that affects every aspect of the business. Context is the world around the organization. Nothing so important as organizational innovation happens in a vacuum. It is obvious that our innovations affect our

customers, suppliers, and competitors in the forms of new products, services, and businesses. But, we also react to shifts in economy, government, technology, and world events as they change the way we view our place in the world. Even our communities and families shape the way our organizations behave. All of these interactions form the context for business activities, including innovation.

Changing Culture

One of the most frequent questions we hear about innovation is "How can we create a culture that supports and sustains innovation?"

The first answer is *You can't.* You don't "create" a culture—it evolves over time through all of the actions, decisions, and behaviors of everyone in the organization. Having the chief executive officer stand up at an annual meeting and say, "We need to be more innovative," will have no effect unless behaviors across the organization change to support the talk. Changing a culture is not as simple as having a training session or putting a bunch of posters on the wall.

The second answer is: *You can but. . . .* It takes time to create a culture. The organization and its leadership have to be willing to focus on the behaviors, systems, and competencies that evolve into culture. You really can't change a culture, but you can change the things that create culture, such as the systems, policies, and internal processes, which means that changing culture is a major undertaking. There is a reason your culture is the way it is: over time it has become the norm of how you act and interact with each other, people have been hired to fit the culture or gradually have adapted to it (or they wind up leaving), and it is the product of years of acting within written and unwritten rules. Therefore, you will not change it overnight. To begin the process, you need to know where to start and what to do first.

By first identifying your Innovation Culture Gap you will know where to start. The Innovation Culture Gap is the difference between the culture you want to create and the culture you currently have.

The InnovationDNA Framework of Innovation Principles presented in the previous chapter can help you identify your culture gaps. Each dimension of the DNA represents the fundamental principles that support innovation. Reviewing this framework will help you understand the complexity of innovation and the importance of doing many things well.

To help you assess your current culture, you can use the Innovation Mini-Audit (in the next chapter) to give you a quick snapshot. Use these questions to stimulate conversation about what is important for your organization and how you're doing in each dimension. You can then focus on the gaps to identify actions that will begin to shift the culture.

What to Do Next

- ◆ Read the next chapter to learn how to use a simple assessment to determine the needs of your organization.

- ◆ Familiarize yourself with the Innovation Mini-Audit. Give it to several of your associates or managers in the organization to begin to get a better sense of your organization's culture.

- ◆ Explore the InnovationNetwork Website, www.thinksmart.com, for more stories and articles about innovation.

◆ ◆ ◆

The next chapter will introduce an innovation mini-audit to help you understand where you should start on your training process to assist your organization in developing greater innovation competency.

Assessing Where to Start

What's in This Chapter?

* Introduction of the innovation Mini-Audit

* Ways to use the Mini-Audit

As is the case with most training interventions, before you can design the optimum program you must know both where you are and where you want to go. Often this means conducting some form of assessment. For innovation training we have developed a simple tool to help you perform this assessment—the Innovation Mini-Audit. It is a concise survey that you can administer to teams, small training groups, and even the entire organization. Before going any farther, it might be beneficial for you to spend a few minutes responding to the survey yourself.

The 14 items in the Innovation Mini-Audit are based on the InnovationDNA and relate directly to the elements of that framework. These items are a synthesis of the kinds of questions we ask in the complete Innovation Audit that assesses an organization's culture and climate for innovation.

The Innovation Mini-Audit provides a snapshot of the cultural environment for innovation. It offers insights that can be used at all three levels of innovation training—organization, team, and individual. At the organization level it can help identify infrastructure issues and cultural barriers to innovation. At the team level it can point to areas that would benefit from training or other interventions for optimum productivity. At the individual level it can raise awareness and spark the realization of personal responsibility for innovation.

Ways to Use the Innovation Mini-Audit

The Innovation Mini-Audit (see Training Instrument 3–1) can serve several purposes for your innovation program:

Training Instrument 3–1

Innovation Mini-Audit

This survey can help you and your top management understand where to start in efforts to increase your organization's innovation capabilities.

Instructions: Using your recent experience with your organization as the basis, please rate the following statements according to the following scale:"

1 = NEVER TRUE	4 = TRUE MOST OF THE TIME
2 = SOMETIMES TRUE	5 = ALWAYS TRUE
3 = FREQUENTLY TRUE	

STATEMENT	RATING
1. Our organization has exciting and interesting challenges that energize us.	1 2 3 4 5
2. My work group understands the importance of innovation to our organization.	1 2 3 4 5
3. We stay abreast of changes in technology, our industry, and the world around us.	1 2 3 4 5
4. People here know who our customers are and understand how their work helps create customer value.	1 2 3 4 5
5. Creative thinking and innovation are important parts of my everyday job.	1 2 3 4 5
6. We have an effective system for capturing, cataloging, and acknowledging new ideas and suggestions.	1 2 3 4 5
7. Our organization openly shares information with employees, customers, and other stakeholders.	1 2 3 4 5
8. People here have opportunities to work with and learn from people in other departments or functional areas.	1 2 3 4 5
9. People here often work on interesting new projects and have developed good project management skills.	1 2 3 4 5
10. We have a defined process of innovation that is widely used throughout the organization.	1 2 3 4 5
11. We regularly review projects, both successful and unsuccessful, to identify lessons learned.	1 2 3 4 5
12. Our leadership provides the encouragement, infrastructure, resources, and support that enables innovation to happen here.	1 2 3 4 5
13. People here have many opportunities to learn and grow.	1 2 3 4 5
14. People here trust and respect each other and generally enjoy working together	1 2 3 4 5

- ◆ To help assess training needs and focus innovation training in your organization

- ◆ To begin to create a picture of your organizational climate for innovation

- ◆ To provide a unique learning activity for a broad audience within your organization.

Using the information garnered from the questions about individuals' jobs (particularly item numbers 2, 4, and 5) you can determine who in the organization should be trained in the various programs we present in this book. Responses to the other 11 items will help you determine the emphasis you might place on the various topics within each program.

A focus on innovation may require your organization to adjust or change in some way. To identify what needs to change or where to begin, a survey like this can be helpful. One way to begin is to have a diverse group of colleagues respond to this mini-audit and then gather them as a group to talk about the responses. The results of a pilot effort like this will help you and your management determine what benefits might be derived from auditing other groups.

For the InnovationDNA overview in chapter 6 we have created a learning activity around the Innovation Mini-Audit. There we connect the 14 items in the audit directly to their respective InnovationDNA elements as a way for participants to understand how the elements come to life in your organization. The Innovation Mini-Audit is informally administered in the workshop setting and participants use it to learn innovation principles and to spark ideas about their own innovation efforts.

If you decide to administer the Innovation Mini-Audit to a broad employee population, you should consider how to manage the overlap with the InnovationDNA overview workshop.

There are other ways to use the audit for training or discussion. The statements in the audit are self-diagnostic in nature so they can help you and others in your organization immediately think about how to improve innovation capabilities and the culture for innovation. Even if the Mini-Audit is not formally administered, each item can serve as a focal point for conversation around innovation. The items are excellent concepts for management groups or innovation champions to explore. As part of your organization's overall innovation efforts, you can become a catalyst and facilitator of these important conversations.

You can host brown-bag lunches where you facilitate conversations around some of the audit items. Ask people to tell stories of innovation efforts they've been involved with. Ask what might help individuals and teams here to be more creative and more innovative. Ask what might hinder these efforts.

For instance, let's say that your organization wants to improve your capabilities around the item, "People here know who our customers are and understand how their work helps to create customer value." You might start by posing the question to groups and then facilitate their brainstorming of ways to help people understand customers better or ways to help everyone understand how customer value is created. Because these are very specific topics that people can get their arms around, participants should be able to generate many good ideas for making improvements.

What to Do Next

- ◆ Become familiar with the InnovationDNA and its elements.

- ◆ Share the InnovationDNA presentation with others.

- ◆ Have a group of people take the Innovation Mini-Audit.

- ◆ Ask people to share stories of innovation in the organization.

- ◆ Read chapters 4 and 6.

◆◆◆

Innovation is the result of competencies that are best developed through a "learning by doing" approach. This means all of the workshops included here intend for new skills to be applied to participants' real work either within the workshops or immediately thereafter. As the facilitator you should also expect to be available to coach. The next chapter speaks to the equation:

New information + Real work + Coaching = New competence.

♦

Beyond Training to Innovation Competency

♦ Discussion of the adult learning model

♦ Introduction of the Innovation Competency Equation

♦ Explanation of your role as facilitator and coach

Why is it that one of the first budgets to be cut in challenging times is training? Everyone *knows* training is important—but the problem is that it is difficult to measure the bottom-line results attributable to training. Management guru Peter Drucker has stated that only marketing and innovation create results for organizations. All other business activities are costs. Therefore, helping people develop greater innovation competency is a training program that can actually produce profit. In this chapter we offer some simple ways to create metrics and feedback systems that will help you solve the problem of validating the results of your training.

The focus of this workbook is on results: the creation of value to your organization as an outgrowth of innovation. The tools and workshops contained here are intended to build innovation competencies that can be demonstrated through the fruits of real work, the outcomes of projects, and the synergies of innovation teams. Oftentimes your follow-up and coaching will make the difference in whether concepts and tools are successfully adopted. And you can measure the impact of your innovation training by tracking the projects or work to which it is applied.

Learning Is in the Doing

It is believed that Confucius once said, "I see and I forget; I hear and I remember; I do and I understand." That ancient wisdom created the foundation for our thinking about adult learning. Twenty-five hundred years later, however, we felt it was time to take Confucius just a bit further. We integrated our years of training into a model we call Confucius Updated: I see possibilities and I show up; I have fun and I am energized; I question and I open the space for learning; I multi-sense and I remember; I do and I understand; I reflect and integrate and I can share with others; I apply to real life and I get results. I teach others and I become a master.

There is little argument in the training world that adults learn best by doing, so the programs outlined here present simulations and action learning approaches. Wherever possible, an action learning model will be used—one that delivers training on a tool that will then be used immediately in a real-work task or project. Because today's organizations do not have much time for people to be doing anything that does not add value to their business, this approach provides an immediate result that can be documented.

The key to successfully institutionalizing innovation tools and practices is to deliver training in a timely—specifically, in a "just-in-time"—manner. Much of training is on a push system—that is, management or "development plans" push training that may seem irrelevant to workers in terms of their everyday responsibilities. The idea of just-in-time training is more of a pull mechanism because workers can see how new skills or tools are relevant in reaching their immediate desired outcomes.

Innovation Competency Equation

Competency is something that must be demonstrated and can be measured. The focus on competency and results speaks directly to the fiscal demands being made on training budgets. Innovation training becomes strategic in its value when it can be linked directly to generating new revenue or profits, cost reduction, or other internal measures of value.

There is a delicate balance between context and content in training designed to deliver improved results. The context—the actual work objectives that dictate the design and facilitation of the training—forms a container that provides the definition and boundaries for the specific content. Providing the necessary theory and background and offering a set of tools or practices are not enough. If the purpose of training is to improve results, the theory and tools must be applied to real work. The bridge between the theory and tools and the actual results is in the application, as well as in the guidance and coaching you provide.

The Competency Equation that forms the foundation for this workbook is

New information + Real work + Coaching = New competence.

Experiential learning offers opportunities for learners to get "Aha's!" Action learning lets them apply the new tools and theories to a real project and thereby create a platform and feedback loop for skill building through timely application. Coaching provides reinforcement and support for ongoing skill integration and evolution. At its best, action learning is a project-based approach through which the organization can realize the value of new competencies in real time. Because it is almost impossible for a wide-audience workbook to direct the application to real work in specific settings, you as the trainer must fill the gap.

We encourage you to find teams working on important innovation projects who would benefit from the innovation tools contained in the workshops we will suggest in later chapters. When they receive the information and tools they need just in time, they will create better results for themselves and your organization. These positive results will create more demand for the training and continue a positive cycle of improvement.

Your Role as Facilitator and Coach

This workbook assumes that your primary roles are as a learning facilitator and a follow-up coach. During the training sessions, the more efficiently you can deliver the informative parts of the training, the better—getting people involved in the interactive parts of the various sessions will be key to your success.

The skill(s) you are transferring in this curriculum will be tested by how individuals and groups approach their innovation challenges as well as their everyday work. These skills are acquired or honed over time so practice and persistence are the true means to mastery. To that end, it is important that you follow up on how people apply their new tools. As a coach you can help those most interested in learning the tools reflect on their experiences, reinforce the process, and continue learning.

If you master the techniques yourself you can become a natural facilitator for strategic innovation teams and innovation project teams. Even if team members can use the tools and techniques themselves, it is often helpful to have a process facilitator so that all team members can fully participate in the content of a thinking session.

What to Do Next

◆ Review chapter 5 to help position your training sessions.

◆ Talk with leaders and managers in your organizations to determine their innovation training needs.

◆◆◆

In many trainings, evaluation by participants ends when they leave the classroom. This is not true of the workshops in this book. In chapter 5, you'll learn about a three-part process to ensure that participants continue to evaluate their learning.

◆

Evaluating and Improving Innovation Training

- ◆ Introduction of a three-part process for measuring the effectiveness of training

- ◆ Explanation of how to use the measurement process

- ◆ Introduction of the measurement tools

- ◆ Discussion about using evaluation feedback

As you know, one of the toughest questions for trainers to answer is "What is the payoff of training?" It's tough because little if any attention is given to posttraining follow up. It is fairly simple to have participants give you their initial reactions when a course or workshop ends, but it is far more difficult to know if the training worked—did participants take the tools and skills back to the workplace and use them effectively? And to imbue training with strategic value we must be able to measure how effectively it aligns with the organization's strategic goals and how it helps workers reach them.

As is true of most training, the value of innovation training is in its successful application on the job. Using classic and fundamental evaluation techniques we have devised a three-part process for evaluating the effectiveness of the innovation training in this workbook. The system is simple and powerful, but it requires you to be disciplined, to invest time, and to create a schedule for follow up after training.

Three-Part Process for Evaluating Innovation Training

Part I of the evaluation is a survey that is filled out when the training event ends. It measures participants' initial impressions of the workshop, with an eye to content relevance, presentation style, and alignment with their expectations.

Part II of the evaluation process—assessing the application of new skills and tools and results of their use—is executed through a "bounce-back," a term borrowed from the advertising world. A bounce-back is a brief questionnaire that you send by email to participants when they are back on the job and have had time to apply their new knowledge or tools.

Part III of the process is notifying supervisors and managers that participants have completed the workshop and asking that they support their workers in applying the knowledge, tools, and skills acquired in training.

Using the Three-Part Process

- ◆ **Preparation:** As part of the registration process for each workshop, make sure you collect the email address of each participant. Also collect the name and email address of each participant's direct supervisor.

- ◆ **Evaluation Part I:** At the end of each workshop, ask participants to complete the Innovation Training Initial Course Evaluation (Training Instrument 5–1) and collect them.

- ◆ **Evaluation Part II, Overview:** After participants have completed the evaluation form, distribute hard copies of the bounce-back questionnaire (Training Instrument 5–2; also available on the accompanying CD) created for the specific workshop. Then do the following:

  1. Explain that this is the second part of the workshop evaluation process, which is intended to help you and the participants determine whether the workshop information and tools or skills are useful on the job.

  2. Explain that in one week you will email this questionnaire to them.

  3. Ask that they respond to it immediately and email it back to you.

  4. Explain that the goal is to get this feedback in order to improve the workshop.

  5. Point out that it is extremely important for everyone to respond to this evaluation request because their responses will trigger the Notice of Completion (Training Instrument 5–3) to be sent to their supervisors.

Training Instrument 5–1

Innovation Training Initial Course Evaluation

Workshop title _____

Date of workshop _____

Thank you for attending today's workshop. Please help us design and deliver training that is of value to you and your colleagues by completing the following survey. To rate your initial reaction to today's learning event, respond to each of the statements below by circling the number that corresponds to the following scale:

1 = TOTALLY DISAGREE	4 = MOSTLY AGREE
2 = MOSTLY DISAGREE	5 = TOTALLY AGREE
3 = GENERALLY AGREE	

STATEMENT	RATING
1. The workshop objectives were clearly explained.	1 2 3 4 5
2. The workshop objectives were achieved.	1 2 3 4 5
3. The workshop met my expectations.	1 2 3 4 5
4. A good learning environment was provided.	1 2 3 4 5
5. I learned new ideas or tools that are applicable to my job.	1 2 3 4 5
6. The workshop leader was prepared.	1 2 3 4 5
7. The workshop leader presented a coherent program.	1 2 3 4 5
8. I felt engaged and involved in the workshop.	1 2 3 4 5
9. I now know more about innovation.	1 2 3 4 5

Comments or suggestions:

*Name*_____ *Department* _____

Training Instrument 5–2

Innovation Training Bounce-Back Questionnaire

Workshop title _____

Date of workshop _____

Thank you for attending the _____ Workshop recently.
Please help us understand how you have been able to apply what you learned
there by completing the following survey and returning it promptly
to _____ at _____ .

1. What key points do you recall from the workshop?

2. What were the ideas that you selected to try?

3. Have you taken the actions you outlined? If so, what results have you noticed thus
    far? If not, please explain if you intend to act and when.

4. What impact, if any, do you think the workshop will have on your work or thinking?

5. What kind of support would help you further use the ideas or tools from the
    workshop?

Other comments:

Name: _____ _Department_ _____

Training Instrument 5–3

Sample Notice of Completion with Instructions for Use

Instructions: When you receive Innovation Training Bounce-Back Questionnaires it is time to send this Notice of Completion with the Certificate of Completion (Training Instrument 5–4) to participants' managers or supervisors via email. Here is a sample Notice that you can use to create your own emails:

To: _____
[manager or supervisor email address]

Subject: **Notice of Completion of Innovation Training**

We are pleased to inform you that _____
[name of participant]

has completed the _____ workshop.
[title of workshop]

Attached is a Certificate of Completion for the workshop. Please present it to

_____ with our congratulations.
[participant's first name]

Thank you.

_____
[Facilitator's signature]

6. Ask participants for a verbal commitment that they will respond to the questionnaire.

◆ **Evaluation Part II and Part III Execution:**

1. One week after the session, email the workshop-specific bounce-back to participants, including a cover note that reiterates the following points:

   a. They should complete and return the questionnaire to you immediately.

   b. Their response is vital to the continued improvement of training in the organization.

   c. When each person's response is received you will send to his or her supervisor a notice of completion of the workshop.

2. Send the notice and the Certificate of Completion Training Instrument 5–4) to the supervisors of those who respond to the bounce- back.

3. Two weeks after the session, repeat steps 1 and 2 for those who did not respond to the first bounce-back.

4. Three weeks after the session, repeat step 1 for those who still have not responded to the first bounce-back. Calculate the response rate for your records. If you are significantly below 75 percent response, you may want to call people to find out why you are not getting their responses.

5. Follow up on responses that indicate significant impact resulting from the training. Develop stories and examples that can be used in future sessions and in training results reports.

6. Share stories and examples with other participants in order to share what has been learned and to encourage further response.

7. Follow up promptly on requests for support.

The Tools

The Initial Course Evaluation form is quite conventional in its nature. This generic tool was designed for use with all of the workshops in this workbook. It asks participants to rate the workshops on the following nine statements:

1. Workshop objectives were clearly explained.

2. Workshop objectives were achieved.

3. The workshop met my expectations.

4. A good learning environment was provided.

5. I learned new ideas or tools that are applicable to my job.

6. The workshop leader was prepared.

7. The workshop leader presented a coherent program.

8. I felt engaged and involved in the workshop.

9. I now know more about innovation.

Training Instrument 5–4

Innovation Training Certificate of Completion

Workshop title _____

Date of workshop _____

To: _____

[name of participant]

Department and Manager: _____

[names of department and direct managers]

We are pleased to announce your completion of the above-named workshop

and we thank you for your post-workshop feedback.

Your contributions to our organization's innovation efforts are appreciated.

_____
Director of Training

_____
Workshop Facilitator

The Bounce-Back Questionnaire is designed to gather information about the application of tools and theories that you have shared with workshop participants. We have designed a generic form for this step, however, you can tailor it for each workshop you present. Here are some general ideas for questions:

1. What key points do you recall from the workshop?

2. What ideas or tools presented in the workshop were most useful to you?

3. Give an example of how you have used (or will use) an idea or tool from the workshop.

4. Can you think of any goals or objectives that the workshop ideas or tools might help you achieve?

5. What kind of support would help you further use the ideas or tools from the workshop?

You can customize the questions to fit your specific workshop designs and organization culture. We recommend, however, that you limit your questionnaires to four or five items.

Using Evaluation Feedback

Innovation occurs in the doing. Although it is important to evaluate the initial reactions of training participants, the feedback gathered in the bounce-back process is more critical to innovation. Are people thinking differently or doing things differently, in ways that might someday result in faster/better/more innovation and measurable value to the organization?

 It is critical to your contribution to innovation that you follow up with participants, especially the first couple of times you offer each of the workshops in this program. Your diligence will likely make a big difference in how many responses you receive. Obviously, the more responses you have to work with, the more reliable your synthesis of the feedback received.

Let's consider the implications of those five sample questions we suggested above:

1. **What key points do you recall from the workshop?** This question should elicit the most varied responses. Different points will resonate with different people depending on their thinking/working styles, function, organization level, and simply personal interests.

You might note if there are key points to which no one responds. If so, consider possible reasons:

- ◆ The point is already well known or ingrained in your organization culture.

- ◆ The point is not viewed as important or relevant in your organization.

- ◆ The point was not well made in the workshop design or delivery. (If you determine that this is the case, re-examine the design and delivery components for improvement.)

2. **What ideas or tools presented in the workshop were most useful to you?** If patterns begin to surface from the responses, you may want to refine the workshop design to focus more on the ideas or tools that people find most useful. Follow up with selected participants and/or their managers to learn more about what other tools would be useful.

3. **Give an example of how you have used (or will use) an idea or tool from the workshop.** Here is the evidence you need to judge the value of the workshop to the participants and, ultimately, to the organization. If people are using the ideas or tools from the workshop, you and the innovation training program have scored a definite victory! If they are not using the ideas or tools, you must take further steps to determine why. Your ultimate response will vary, depending on whether the problem lies in content or training, is a cultural issue, or is one of management or leadership.

4. **Can you think of any goals or objectives that the workshop ideas or tools might help you achieve?** This kind of question is probably not appropriate for some of the one-hour programs. Where it is appropriate, however, the responses might help you in designing new innovation workshops and in following up with those participants who want to learn more.

5. **What kind of support would help you further use the ideas or tools from the workshop?** Like the previous question, the responses here can help guide you to new offerings, including

the creation of coaching or mentoring programs. These responses can also provide management with information about where infrastructure, processes, and practices can be enhanced to grease the wheels for more innovation.

As a trainer you are experienced with evaluation techniques, and your organization likely has its own style. We trust you will modify and customize our suggested formats.

◆◆◆

So, enough about getting ready! The first workshop is outlined in chapter 6: InnovationDNA—One-Hour Overview.

InnovationDNA—One-Hour Overview Workshop

What's in This Chapter?

- Discussion of ways to get your organization started on innovation

- Information on objectives, target audience, materials, and preparations for the InnovationDNA One-Hour Overview Workshop

- Detailed agenda for the workshop

- Instructions for conducting the workshop

One of the underpinnings of innovation is making context—the big picture—explicit for individuals and the organization as a whole. It is important that everyone have a general sense of what innovation is and of its potential impact on your collective future. Because innovation is such a huge and complex system, it is helpful to provide a systematic way to understand the pieces and parts of innovation and to help everyone see how they fit into it.

In chapter 2 we introduced the InnovationDNA. This thinking framework offers a common language and way of getting one's arms around the concept of organizational innovation. Using the InnovationDNA, you can begin to institutionalize the concepts, practices, and mindset of innovation in your organization. The one-hour workshop presented in this chapter is a concise introduction to innovation that is appropriate for people at all levels and involved in all functions.

You will probably want to consult with your top management or the sponsors of your innovation initiative to identify the various audiences for this workshop and to determine how to invite those people. It is likely to be beneficial to participants if groups are somewhat mixed so that everyone is exposed to a diversity of opinions and thinking styles. The topic of innovation and this workshop are a great way to open up communication about the organization and its future success.

Training Objectives

The objectives of the InnovationDNA One-Hour Overview Workshop are to

- present a brief overview of innovation

- stimulate discussion about organizational strengths and opportunities for improvement relative to innovation

- stimulate thinking about how individuals can affect those strengths and challenges.

Target Audience

The target audience for this workshop includes everyone in the organization who should understand the basic concepts of innovation.

Materials

For the facilitator:

- Four or five poster-sized copies of the InnovationDNA graphic for the walls

- Eight to 10 stimulating quotes or inspirational photos mounted on colored paper for the walls

- InnovationDNA PowerPoint presentation (*InnovationDNA.ppt*).

- InnovationDNA suggested script to accompany the PowerPoint slides (Tool 6–1)

- Laptop computer

- LCD projector and screen

For the participants:

- One color copy of the InnovationDNA graphic for each participant. (The color version of the InnovationDNA can be printed on a color printer from the Figure 6–2.pdf file on the accompanying CD.)

- One copy of the Dimensions of the InnovationDNA Model (Handout 11–15)

◆ One copy of the Innovation Mini-Audit Exercise (Tool 6–2)

◆ One copy of the Initial Course Evaluation (Training Instrument 5–1)

◆ One copy of the Bounce-Back Questionnaire (Training Instrument 5–2)

◆ Pen or pencil for each participant

Using the CD

Some materials for this training session are provided in this workbook and as electronic files on the accompanying CD. To access the electronic files, insert the CD and click on the appropriate Adobe .pdf document. Further directions and help locating and using the files can be found in the appendix, "Using the Compact Disc."

Room Logistics

This session will work best for both activities and timing if people are seated at tables in groups of four.

Preparation

To prepare for the workshop, review the InnovationDNA principles outlined in chapter 2 and the PowerPoint presentation on the CD. You will be showing those PowerPoint slides as part of the workshop. Also review the Innovation Mini-Audit in chapter 3. Workshop participants will complete the Innovation Mini-Audit Exercise (Tool 6–2), which includes group work.

One-Hour InnovationDNA Overview Workshop Sample Agenda

Figure 6–1 is a condensed black-and-white version of the complete map for this workshop, which is available on the CD (see Figure 6–2.pdf)

7:30 a.m.   Room Preparation

Make sure the room is organized, neat, and inviting.

Hang poster-sized graphics, quotes, and inspirational images or artwork on the walls.

Figure 6–1

InnovationDNA Overview Workshop Map

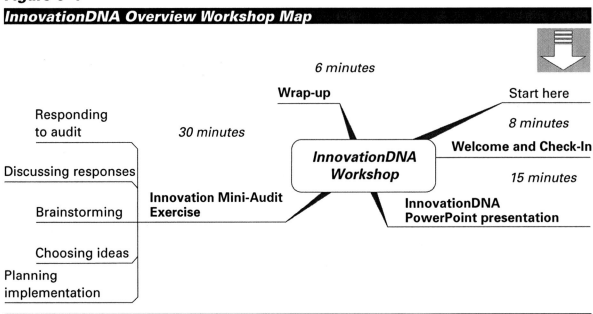

At each participant's seat, place

◆ a color copy of InnovationDNA graphic (Figure 2–2.pdf on the CD)

◆ a copy of Dimensions of the InnovationDNA Model (Handout 11–15)

◆ an Innovation Mini-Audit Exercise (Tool 6–2)

8:00   Welcome (5 minutes)

Welcome participants to the workshop, introduce yourself, and explain what you hope to accomplish in the session:

◆ to give them a broad overview of how innovation works in organizations

◆ to give them a common language for innovation

◆ to stimulate discussion about the strengths and opportunities for improvement within the organization relative to innovation and how individuals can affect those strengths and opportunities.

8:05   Check-In (3 minutes)

8:08   InnovationDNA Overview PowerPoint Presentation (*InnovationDNA.ppt*, 15 minutes)

8:23   Give participants 5 to 7 minutes to complete the Innovation Mini-Audit Exercise, steps 1, 2, and 3.

8:30   (Step 4) Give participants 10 minutes to share in their pairs which items they chose in steps 2 and 3 of the audit and why—what they rank highest and lowest. (Give them a time warning at 8 or 9 minutes to be sure everyone has a chance to share.)

        Pass out the Initial Course Evaluation and the Bounce-Back Questionnaire while they are completing this step.

8:40   (Step 5) Give participants 3 minutes to individually generate some ideas of how they or their co-workers might help leverage the strength identified in step 2 (the item they rate highest).

8:43   (Step 6) Give participants 3 minutes to generate ideas individually for how they or their co-workers could help improve the item they rated lowest in step 3.

8:46   (Step 7) Give participants 1 minute to look over the ideas they generated in steps 5 and 6 and then choose one idea they would be willing to act on.

8:47   (Step 8) Confirm that each person has chosen one idea. Ask them to write down the first one or two action steps to take to implement that idea. (2 minutes)

8:49   Ask participants to complete the Initial Course Evaluation. (3 minutes)

8:52   Ask participants to share with their partners the idea they chose and the action steps they intend to take. (5 minutes)

8:57   Explain the Bounce-Back Questionnaire and the Notice of Completion process. (2 minutes)

        Note that the course is not complete until they determine its value on the job. Tell them that you will email the questionnaire to them in 7 to 10 days, and that when they respond you will send the Notice of Completion and a Certificate of Completion to their managers or supervisors.

Ask for **commitment** (by show of hands) to respond to the Bounce-Back Questionnaire when they receive it.

8:59   Thank **participants** and encourage them to follow through **on** their ideas to help your organization become more innovative.

 ## What to Do Next

- ◆ Compile the handouts, slides, and other materials to be used in the training.

- ◆ Determine the schedule and room logistics for the class(es).

- ◆ Determine how participants will be invited.

- ◆ Invite participants.

◆ ◆ ◆

The next chapter outlines a series of one-hour workshops that will enable your entire organization to understand the principles of innovation.

Tool 6–1
InnovationDNA Overview Suggested PowerPoint Script

SLIDE NUMBER	REFERENCE	BACKGROUND	SCRIPT
1	Title page		
2	What Is InnovationDNA?	InnovationDNA presents a set of principles concerning how innovation occurs in organizations. It is the result of the study of many organizations . . . organizations as diverse as Cirque du Soliel, 3M, and CSX Transportation. The Founding Fellows of the InnovationNetwork program called InnovationUniversity created the original metaphor of the helix as the operational dimensions of innovation. The framework has evolved over the years as InnovationNetwork has continued to observe how organizations around the world innovate. InnovationDNA is a synthesis of the principles and practices observed in these organizations with the latest thinking on innovation from a broad spectrum of innovation practitioners and authors.	This is a brief overview of the InnovationDNA framework, which presents a way of organizing our thinking around the huge concept of innovation. InnovationDNA was originally conceived in the mid-90s by a group of businesspeople who did in-depth study of how various organizations approached innovation. It continues to evolve as business and industry change and more information is gathered. We are using InnovationDNA to help [*insert your organization's name*] learn about innovation and to help deploy our strategy to be more innovative by establishing a common language and thinking framework.
3	Why Innovation?	Although it is always important, innovation has recently become the focal point of many organizations' strategies. The accelerating speed of change in both business and technology have forced organizations to look to innovation as a crucial path for future growth and prosperity.	There are many reasons to innovate. What are they? [*Class responds with ideas that you capture on flipchart paper. Encourage participants to offer five to eight ideas if possible. Summarize this slide by clicking through and reading the three general points contained.*]

continued on next page

Tool 6–1, continued

InnovationDNA Overview Suggested PowerPoint Script

SLIDE NUMBER	REFERENCE	BACKGROUND	SCRIPT
4	What Is Innovation?	Many organizations create their own definitions of innovation. Does yours have one? If so, how widely is this known?	So, what is innovation? Do you have ideas on how we define it here? [*Look for three to four responses.*]
5	Innovation Is:	This definition is one simple version of the general thinking of authors and practitioners working with organizations to innovate. In the early 90s there was some confusion about the difference between creativity and innovation. Whereas creativity is the way novel ideas come to light, the concept of creativity does not demand implementation. One could argue that in the pure sense, innovation is simply the implementation of new ideas. In the context of business—whether for profit or not for profit—all activities, including innovation, must deliver value.	InnovationDNA's definition is people implementing new ideas that create value. Please notice that there are three key components of this definition: 1. New ideas 2. People implementing them 3. Value is realized by an external or internal customer through implemented ideas
6	Three Parts	At the big-picture level InnovationDNA has three main parts. The outer arc (purple) is the Context—it represents the world outside our organizations. Innovation is closely related to the outside world—if we didn't have competitors, or if we didn't know what was going on in industry, or if the government didn't force regulations, would we innovate in the same way?	Innovation is a big concept—it's really a system that includes the entire organization. Please follow along on your handouts and we will walk through the InnovationDNA, beginning with the big picture. There are three main parts of this framework: 1. The purple outer arc represents the larg-

continued on next page

Tool 6–1, continued

InnovationDNA Overview Suggested PowerPoint Script

SLIDE NUMBER	REFERENCE	BACKGROUND	SCRIPT
		The black arc is the second main part of the framework—it represents organizational culture. As you well know, culture affects practically everything that happens in an organization, including both how well and how easily it innovates. The third area of the framework is the helix, which is a metaphor for the operational aspects of innovation. It speaks to how creativity, communication, collaboration, and other factors drive the actual process of innovation.	er context for innovation—the outside world. 2. The black arc depicts organizational culture. 3. The green DNA helix delineates the operational aspects of innovation. Let's look at each part a little closer by examining where and how innovation happens
7	Where Innovation Happens—Context		Nothing within our organization happens in a vacuum, including innovation. At the macro level, the context for innovation is the outside world.
8	Context for Innovation		The way we as individuals and as an organization interact with the outside world creates the larger context for innovation. [*Begin clicking through the key influencers— Click Customers, Suppliers, Competitors*] It's easy for all of us to see how our customers, suppliers, and competitors affect us every day. [*Click Economy, Government and World Events*] Even if we don't have direct contact,

continued on next page

Tool 6–1, continued

InnovationDNA Overview Suggested PowerPoint Script

SLIDE NUMBER	REFERENCE	BACKGROUND	SCRIPT
			it's easy to see how the economy, the government, and world events affect our business.
			[*Click Community and Family*] And, of course, our community and even individual families affect our organization and everything it does.
9	Where Innovation Happens—Culture		Looking strictly inside our organization, the playing field for innovation is our Culture.
10	Culture	The study or analysis of an organization's culture is critical to understanding how to promote or enhance innovation within it. Here are some of questions an organization can ask about its culture and whether there are barriers to innovation: Is it the culture's natural tendency to listen to ideas? Is information openly and widely shared? Do people feel free to speak their minds? Do people take calculated risks to advance great, new ideas that will benefit the organization? Does the organization value curiosity and learning? Do people trust and respect each other?	Culture includes the shared beliefs, behavioral norms, and traditions of an organization. Culture has a huge influence on how an organization innovates. There are four key components of culture that drive innovation. [*Click through and name the four items.*] Let's look at each of these four components and some examples that will help bring these concepts to life.
11	Culture: Leadership	There is usually an evolution of leadership awareness that leads to actions to advance innovation. As the buzz of innovation grew throughout the 90s, many prominent organi-	It is leadership's job to look to the future, identify opportunities, and prepare and support our organization to capture those opportunities. [*Click for the example*]

continued on next page

Tool 6–1, continued

InnovationDNA Overview Suggested PowerPoint Script

SLIDE NUMBER	REFERENCE	BACKGROUND	SCRIPT
		zations' top leadership talked about innovation. However, it often took several years before that talk translated into strategy and then into tactics that would produce real results. Awareness and education are often the first steps toward increasing innovation, no matter where you are on the organizational chart!	Air Products and Chemicals, Inc., a specialty chemical company, wants to make sure they stay on track in their new innovation efforts. So they created the position of director of innovation and early business development. Having a high-level person focused solely on innovation demonstrates their commitment to innovation.
12	Culture: People	Just as nothing happens in a vacuum, nothing happens without people.	It's really true that people are the most significant part of innovation. Not only are people's ideas important, but how people interact and work together is critical to innovation. [*Click*] The Neenan Company is a real estate development, construction, and management company. Their people spend inordinate amounts of time and effort actively building trust and relationships with customers, suppliers, each other, and their community. One of their core values is love.
13	Culture: Basic Values	Of the basic values, there are some to which most organizations subscribe: trust, integrity, learning, commitment, success, and honesty. Some other values that are important to innovation, however, are not as often embraced or	Basic values are those shared widely throughout the organization that tend to mold actions like how business is conducted, how decisions are made, and how people treat each other. Some values that seem to influence innovation are trust, learning, openness, commit-

continued on next page

Tool 6-1, continued

InnovationDNA Overview Suggested PowerPoint Script

SLIDE NUMBER	REFERENCE	BACKGROUND	SCRIPT
		articulated-values such as honoring risk, openness, and inclusiveness.	ment, contribution, inclusiveness, and honoring risk. What are some basic values we have here? [*Look for five to seven ideas/responses.*]
14	Culture: Innovation Values		There are some organizations that seem to have something special about them that helps them be more creative and innovative than most others. Some of those special qualities or values are listed here under Innovation Values. They include freedom, intuition, passion, and fun! [*Click*] At the advertising agency GSD&M their core values are literally engraved in stone in the rotunda of their building, which is called Idea City. The values engraved include restlessness, freedom and responsibility, and curiosity.
15	How Does Innovation Happen?		Innovation happens when organizations are in touch with the outside world, their cultures support it, and there are practices and processes in place to make it so.
16	The Helix		Innovation requires that many pieces of process and practice come together. The helix, in green on the graphic, depicts seven main

continued on next page

Tool 6–1, continued

InnovationDNA Overview Suggested PowerPoint Script

SLIDE NUMBER	REFERENCE	BACKGROUND	SCRIPT
			dimensions. We'll look at each of them individually and at some examples.
			It all starts down there at the bottom of the helix with a new idea, a new trend, or some kind of change.
17	Challenge		Innovation is inspired by a challenge that is compelling and perhaps pulls at the heart. Challenge provides energy for the pursuit. [*Click*]
			Interface Americas, one of the largest carpet manufacturers in the world, has challenged itself to clean up its industry and prevent carpet from going into landfills. This challenge causes them to find solutions other than disposal for reuse or recycle of materials.
18	Customer Focus		In the past we relied solely on conventional market research to provide direction for new products or businesses. With the growth of ethnographic research, companies are getting to know their end-users very well. [*Click*]
			Datex-Ohmeda, a medical device company, began doing ethnographic research and created a process called Discovery to create a discipline in this work within the organization.

continued on next page

Tool 6-1, continued
InnovationDNA Overview Suggested PowerPoint Script

SLIDE NUMBER	REFERENCE	BACKGROUND	SCRIPT
19	Creativity		Everything starts with an idea. And most people have ideas they can offer to their organization. One way to make everyone part of the process is to run idea campaigns around important issues. Creativity is not about art; it's thinking creatively—finding new ways to connect disparate thoughts. [*Click*]
			Rohm and Haas, the chemical company, sends teams out into unlikely places to look for new ideas or sparks for creativity.
20	Communication		Communication is truly the lifeblood of any organization. Innovation cannot happen unless people are communicating their thinking, experiences, and ideas to each other.
			Organizations that think together will naturally be creating the raw material for innovation. [*Click*]
			World Bank has discovered the power of stories as a way to communicate. They now create and tell stories all over the world that inform, inspire, and educate.
21	Collaboration		In today's organizations it is practically impossible to produce results on one's own; almost everything is a team effort. Collaboration is a

continued on next page

Tool 6–1, continued

InnovationDNA Overview Suggested PowerPoint Script

SLIDE NUMBER	REFERENCE	BACKGROUND	SCRIPT
			key principle of innovation—it takes a team to ensure that ideas are developed and implemented. [*Click*]
			True collaboration is often scarce within a single organization, much less across organizations. Orange juice maker Tropicana Products, Inc. and their rail transportation supplier CSX had an adversarial relationship for more than 25 years. By building trust and respect they have created a cross-company innovation team that has brought millions of dollars to the top and bottom lines.
22	Completion		Implementation of ideas usually means mounting a project and managing it through its completion. Project management skills and tools are essential to innovation. Sound processes, good decision making, and careful monitoring are key. [*Click*]
			Citigroup created a Rapid Approval team to make sure that ideas moved forward quickly and had the support they needed.
23	Contemplation		Life and business are extremely busy. However, reflection is a crucial part of learning and innovating. Capturing the lessons learned

continued on next page

Tool 6–1, continued

InnovationDNA Overview Suggested PowerPoint Script

SLIDE NUMBER	REFERENCE	BACKGROUND	SCRIPT
			from both success and failure is important. Sharing those lessons throughout the organization creates a collective wisdom. [*Click*]
			Pillsbury, which is now part of General Mills, created project summaries they called Learning Histories as part of their knowledge management.
			What are the ways we capture and share lessons here? [*Allow time for two to four responses.*]
24	Innovation Is Both an Art and a Science		At its essence innovation is very simple. But it is quite complicated to execute. The way we see the world, our culture, mindset, processes, and practices all come together to make innovation happen.
			It is important that our entire organization understands innovation and how to contribute to it.
			[*End of slide presentation*]

Tool 6–2

Innovation Mini-Audit Exercise

Name _____

Date _____

This survey, based on the InnovationDNA, can help our organization understand where to start in efforts to increase our innovation capabilities.

Step 1: Please respond to each statement based on your recent experience here:

1 = NEVER TRUE	4 = TRUE MOST OF THE TIME
2 = SOMETIMES TRUE	5 = ALWAYS TRUE
3 = FREQUENTLY TRUE	

DNA ELEMENT	STATEMENT	RATING	+/–
Challenge	1. Our organization has exciting and interesting challenges that energize us.	1 2 3 4 5	
Culture: Values	2. My workgroup understands the importance of innovation to our organization.	1 2 3 4 5	
Context: World	3. We stay abreast of changes in technology, our industry and the world around us.	1 2 3 4 5	
Customer Focus	4. People here know who our customers are and understand how their work helps to create customer value.	1 2 3 4 5	
Creativity	5. Creative thinking and innovation are an important part of my everyday job.	1 2 3 4 5	
Creativity	6. We have an effective system for capturing, cataloging, and acknowledging new ideas and suggestions.	1 2 3 4 5	
Communication	7. Our organization openly shares information with employees, customers, and other stakeholders.	1 2 3 4 5	
Collaboration	8. People here have opportunities to work with and learn from people in other departments or functional areas.	1 2 3 4 5	
Completion	9. People here often work on interesting new projects and have developed good project management skills.	1 2 3 4 5	
Completion	10. We have a defined process of innovation that is widely used throughout the organization.	1 2 3 4 5	
Contemplation	11. We regularly review projects, both successful and unsuccessful, in order to identify lessons learned.	1 2 3 4 5	

continued on next page

Tool 6–2, continued
Innovation Mini-Audit Exercise

DNA ELEMENT	STATEMENT	RATING	+/–
Culture: Leadership	12. Our leadership provides the encouragement, infrastructure, resources and support for innovation to happen here.	1 2 3 4 5	
Culture: People	13. People here have many opportunities to learn and grow.	1 2 3 4 5	
Culture: Values	14. People here trust and respect each other and generally enjoy working together.	1 2 3 4 5	

Step 2: Mark a "+" in the right-hand column next to the item that you would rate the highest. (You may have to choose among several that you rated equally on the 1–5 scale.)

Step 3: Mark a "–" in the right-hand column next to the item that you would rate the lowest. (You may have to choose among several that you rated equally on the 1–5 scale.)

Step 4: With your thinking partner(s), share your choices for Steps 2 and 3 and the reasons behind your choices. (You'll have 12–15 minutes for you and your partners to share your thinking.)

Step 5: Working by yourself for two minutes, generate ideas on how you could help your organization leverage the strength you identified in Step 2—the item you marked with a "+" above. (Jot your ideas here.)

Step 6: Working by yourself for two minutes, generate ideas on how you could help your organization improve on the item you identified in Step 3—the item you marked with a "–" above. (Jot your ideas here.)

Step 7: From among the ideas you generated in Steps 5 and 6, choose one that you would be willing to try. Circle that idea.

Step 8: Identify the first action to take to implement the idea you selected and decide when you will take it. Note those below:

*What I will do first:*_____

*When I will do it:*_____

Slide 6–1

InnovationDNA ™

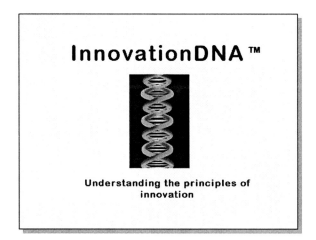

Understanding the principles of
innovation

Slide 6–2

 **InnovationDNA:
A framework of
principles**
• Provides common
language
• Organizes thinking
• Provides a conceptual
anchor

Slide 6–3

Why innovation?

**To create new
products/services**

To ensure growth

**To stay abreast of
the world and our
industry**

Slide 6–4

**What is
innovation?**

Slide 6–5

Innovation is:

People implementing

    new ideas

        that create value

Slide 6–6

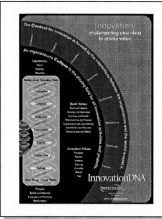

**Three
parts**

•Context
• Culture
• Operational
dimensions

Slide 6–7

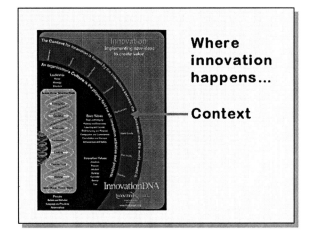

Slide 6–8

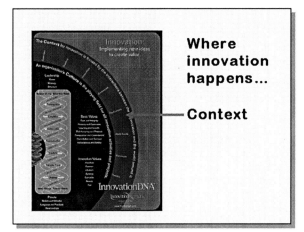

Slide 6–9

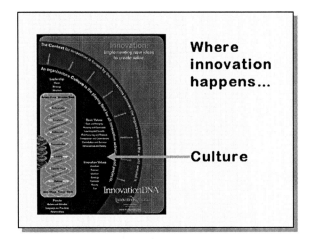

Slide 6–10

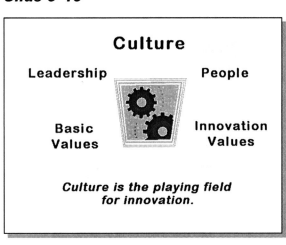

Slide 6–11

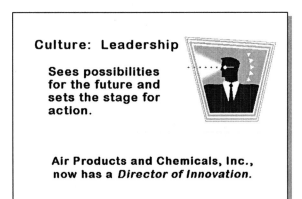

Slide 6–12

Culture: People

Relationships and how people interact with each other.

At The Neenan Company, coworkers take great pains to create "intentional" relationships with each other.

Slide 6–13

Culture: Basic Values

Define and distinguish an organization.

What are some of the core values in our organization?

Slide 6–14

Culture: Innovation Values

Stoke the fires that make the impossible possible.

GSD&M has engraved their values in stone...including the innovation value Curiosity.

Slide 6–15

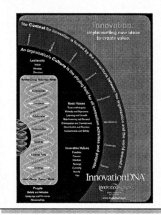

How does innovation happen?

Slide 6–16

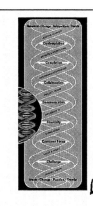

The Helix:

7 operational dimensions of innovation.

The entry way...ideas, a passion, winds of change

Slide 6–17

Challenge excites people and creates energy and alignment.

Interface Americas, Inc., wants to create zero waste and restore the environment.

Slide 6–18

Customer Focus: Creating value for customers is the purpose of innovation.

Datex-Ohmeda started Discovery to learn about customers first-hand.

Slide 6–19

Creativity: It's important to make everyone part of the idea process.

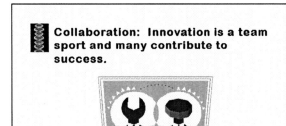

Rohm and Haas searches the world for ideas.

Slide 6–20

Communication of ideas, information, and experiences is vital.

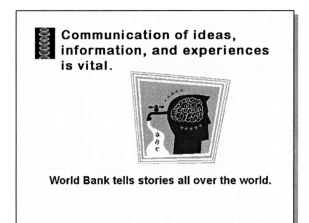

World Bank tells stories all over the world.

Slide 6–21

Collaboration: Innovation is a team sport and many contribute to success.

CSX & Tropicana tore down a 25-year-old wall.

Slide 6–22

Completion happens through effective project management.

CitiGroup's Rapid Approval team builds ideas instead of killing them.

Slide 6–23

Contemplation is gleaning and sharing lessons learned.

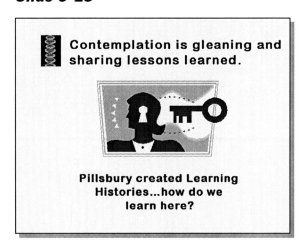

Pillsbury created Learning Histories...how do we learn here?

Slide 6–24

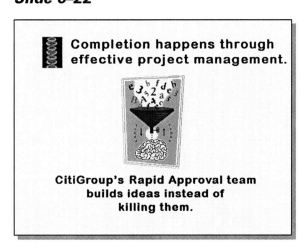

Innovation is both art and science. It is both chaotic and disciplined.

It is a complex system that involves the entire organization.

◆

Innovation Comes Alive!— One-Hour Programs

- ◆ Design for a series of one-hour programs focusing on different aspects of InnovationDNA

- ◆ Overview map of the workshop

- ◆ Eight variations that match elements of the InnovationDNA

- ◆ Detailed program agenda that can be used for each session of the series

- ◆ Instructions for conducting each program

- ◆ Bounce-back questionnaire for the workshop series

This chapter includes a short program that can be used as an introduction to innovation. As a one-hour presentation, it can be used as a brown-bag lunch program or as part of a staff-training session or meeting. One sample agenda is provided with indications for specific learning activities to fit each element of the InnovationDNA.

Training Objectives

The objectives of the Innovation Comes Alive! Workshop are to

- ◆ present an overview of innovation

- ◆ stimulate discussion about the principles of innovation.

Target Audience

The target audience for this workshop includes anyone who wants a broad understanding of innovation.

Materials

For the facilitator:

- ◆ Four or five poster-sized InnovationDNA graphics for the wall

- ◆ Small toys; avoid any toys that make noise

- ◆ Eight to 10 stimulating quotes printed on 8.5 x 11-inch colored paper for the wall

- ◆ Learning Activity 10–1 and your choice of Learning Activity 10–2 through 10–9

- ◆ InnovationDNA PowerPoint presentation (*InnovationDNA.ppt*)

- ◆ Laptop computer and LCD projector with screen

For the participants:

- ◆ One color copy of the InnovationDNA graphic for each participant (Tool 6–2.pdf on the CD)

- ◆ Colored pens and paper

- ◆ Sticky notes for some activities

- ◆ Yellow index cards for some activities

- ◆ One Innovation Training Initial Course Evaluation with workshop title and date completed for each person (Training Instrument 5–1)

- ◆ One Innovation Training Bounce-Back Questionnaire with workshop title and date completed for each person (Training Instrument 5–2)

Using the CD

Some materials for this training session are provided in this workbook and as electronic files on the accompanying CD. To access the electronic files, insert the CD and click on the appropriate Adobe .pdf document. Further directions and help locating and using the files can be found in the appendix, "Using the Compact Disc."

Room Logistics

These sessions work best when participants sit at tables in groups of four to six people. That arrangement facilitates writing and conversation.

Figure 7–1
Innovation Comes Alive! Workshop Map

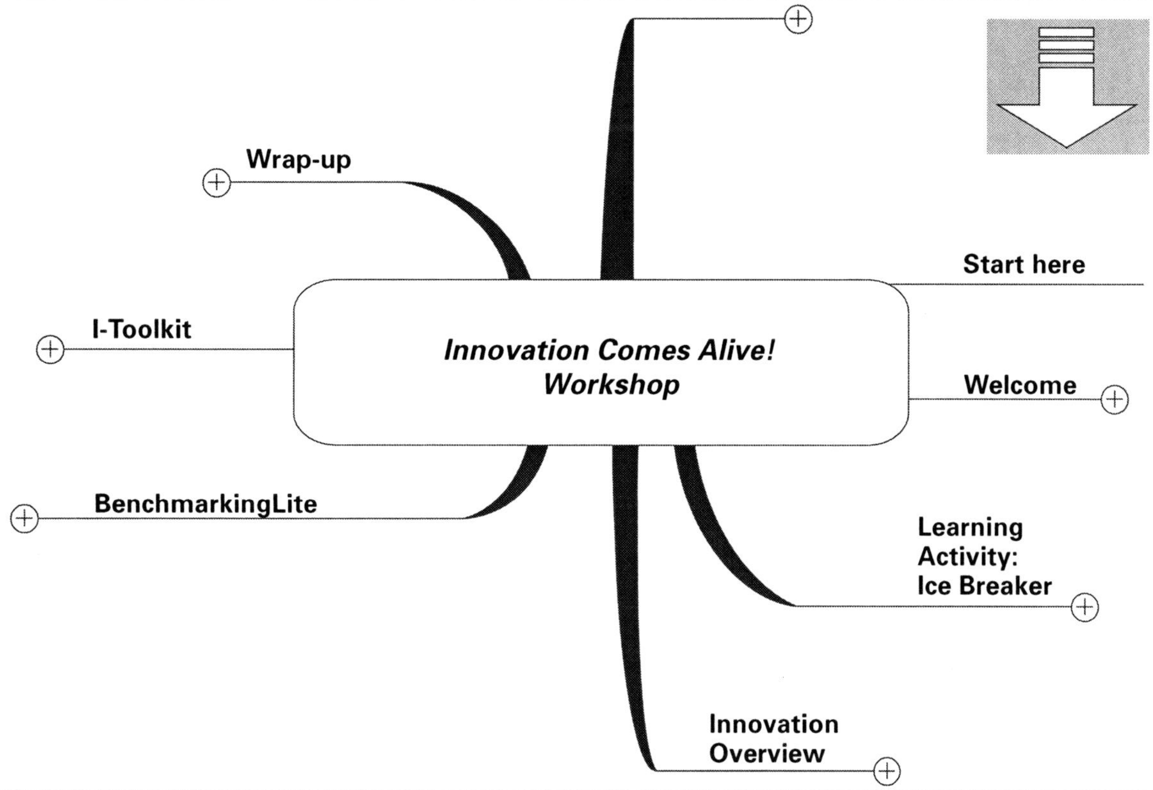

Wrap-up

I-Toolkit

Innovation Comes Alive! Workshop

BenchmarkingLite

Start here

Welcome

Learning Activity: Ice Breaker

Innovation Overview

Preparation

To prepare for the workshop, review the InnovationDNA principles outlined in chapter 2 and the PowerPoint presentation on the CD. You will be showing those PowerPoint slides as part of the workshop.

One-Hour Innovation Comes Alive! Sample Agenda

Figure 7–1 is a condensed black-and-white version of the complete map for this workshop, which is available on the CD (see Figure 7–2.pdf).

    7:30 a.m.   Room Preparation

                 Make sure the room is organized, neat, and inviting.

                 Place a copy of the InnovationDNA graphic at each participant's place.

On the wall hang poster-sized copies of the InnovationDNA graphic as well as the stimulating quotes you have chosen.

Sprinkle small toys around the tables to help create a fresh and fun mindset.

Place a dish of candies in the center of each table to sweeten the environment and provide a small mental boost.

8:00   Welcome (5 minutes)

Welcome participants to the program, introduce yourself, and provide information about why the program is being offered and what you hope to accomplish.

8:05   Ice Breakers (10 minutes)

Facilitate whatever activity in Learning Activity 10–1 matches the innovation element you are focusing on for this program. These activities are designed to break the ice, stimulate conversation around innovation, and begin the learning process. The various activities are

- Culture: What's Your Thinking Style (Learning Activity 10–1A)

- Challenge: Wouldn't It Be Great If. . . ? (Learning Activity 10–1B)

- Customer Focus: Customer Archetype Story (Learning Activity 10–1C)

- Creativity: Innovation Here Is Like... (Learning Activity 10–1D)

- Communication: Innovation Story (Learning Activity 10–1E)

- Collaboration: Dream Team (Learning Activity 10–1F)

- Completion: Best Failure Story (Learning Activity 10–1G)

- Contemplation: Learning and Teaching Offers (Learning Activity 10–1H)

8:15   Innovation Overview (10 minutes)

Present the definition of innovation, emphasizing each of its four components:

Innovation is people creating value by implementing new ideas.

1. **People:** innovation is done only by people, and generally only by groups of people working collaboratively. They may engage technology and other resources in the process of innovation, but machines can't innovate . . . at least not yet.

2. **Creating value:** the purpose of innovation is to create value for the customer (internal or external), and for the organization community, or other stakeholder.

3. **Implementing:** innovation isn't finished until there is a result, whether that's a new process, product, service, delivery mechanism, business model, or system.

4. **New ideas:** innovation requires new ideas, new ways of looking at problems and opportunities. Ideas are gossamer pieces of fluff without value by themselves, but woven together with purpose and skill, they become the stuff of legends.

    Present the InnovationDNA overview PowerPoint slides, which briefly explain each element of the DNA (*InnovationDNA.ppt;* see black-and-white thumbnail versions of the slides at the end of chapter 6).

8:25   I-Toolkit (25 minutes)

Facilitate whichever learning activity matches the InnovationDNA element you are focusing on in this program. This activity gives people a simple, specific tool that they can use when they return to the workplace.

*   **Culture:** Springboard Stories (Learning Activity 10–2)

*   **Challenge:** Cracking Questions (Learning Activity 10–3)

- ◆ **Customer Focus:** Breakthrough Generator (Learning Activity 10–4)

- ◆ **Creativity:** BrainwritingPlus (Learning Activity 10–5)

- ◆ **Communication:** Think 360 (Learning Activity 10–6)

- ◆ **Collaboration:** Quadrant Collaboration (Learning Activity 10–7)

- ◆ **Completion:** Innovation Criteria Grid (Learning Activity 10–8)

- ◆ **Contemplation:** Contemplation Matrix (Learning Activity 10–9)

8:50   Wrap-Up (10 minutes)

Facilitate a discussion of questions and insights. Ask people to write down on their yellow index cards one activity that might spark new innovative action that they could do when they return to their workplace. Ask people to read what they've written and ask listeners who hear something they might also like to do to write it on their cards also.

9:00   Close

Thank people for coming and encourage them to attend future sessions on other elements of innovation.

What to Do Next

- ◆ Prepare for the series of one-hour sessions.

- ◆ Compile the learning activities, handouts, and PowerPoint presentations that will be used in the training.

- ◆ Determine the schedule and room logistics for the classes.

- ◆ Invite participants.

◆ ◆ ◆

The next chapter offers a three-hour workshop that will help participants understand how to use creativity tools to generate and evaluate ideas.

Creativity Made Simple— Three-Hour Workshop

- ◆ Design for a three-hour creativity workshop

- ◆ Explanation of the purpose and objectives for the program

- ◆ Notes on delivery and transitions

- ◆ Overview map of the workshop

- ◆ Detailed sample program agenda

- ◆ Instructions for conducting the workshop

- ◆ Bounce-back questionnaire for the workshop

Creativity can seem like magic...and it is...but it can also be demystified by understanding its intrinsic phases and underlying principles plus one very important rule. This important rule is to always separate divergent thinking and convergent thinking into discreet activities. This chapter provides you with a sample format for a three-hour creativity program. You may use the format as is or create your own session by choosing different activities from chapter 10 or combining activities from this book with your own.

This program format works well for people who need a comprehensive overview of creativity and the experience of using some of the simple but powerful tools that can help people generate more and better ideas.

Training Objectives

The objectives of the Creativity Made Simple Workshop are to

- ◆ understand the fundamentals of creative thinking

- ◆ learn to use simple, powerful tools to enhance creative thinking

    ◆ learn to develop an engaging challenge statement

    ◆ understand different thinking styles

    ◆ practice generating ideas

    ◆ practice selecting best ideas

Target Audience

This workshop is ideal for anyone who wants to understand creativity and how to generate more and better ideas by using simple but powerful tools.

Materials

For the facilitator:

    ◆ Name tags

    ◆ Basket or bowl, relatively large

    ◆ Colored construction paper—red, green, yellow—one of each color per table

    ◆ Paper cutter or several pairs of scissors if a cutter is not available

    ◆ Scotchtape, one roll per table

    ◆ Large manila envelope marked "Red Ideas"

    ◆ Easel, large pad of paper, and marking pens

    ◆ Colored dots (each sheet should have rows of red, green, blue, and yellow dots; these are available at office supply stores), one sheet per eight people

    ◆ Small red dots, supplied on sheets or rolls, enough for every participant to have three dots

    ◆ Images from magazines, at least five to 10 images per attendee. Choose interesting or intriguing images: people or animals in action or in unusual situations; anything that sparks curiosity, mystery, or a strong response.

    ◆ Learning Activity 10–1: What's Your Thinking Style?

    ◆ Learning Activity 10–10: Are You Creative?

- Learning Activity 10–5: BrainwritingPlus

- Learning Activity 10–3: Cracking Questions

- Learning Activity 10–6: Think 360

- Learning Activity 10–11: Three-Color Sorting

- Refreshments for break

For the participants:

- 4 x 6-inch Sticky notes, two pads per table

- Handout 11–1: What's Your Thinking Style?

- Handout 11–13: Creativity Made Simple: SWAMI SOARS!

- Handout 11–6: Better Brainstorming Guidelines

- Handout 11–7: BrainwritingPlus Worksheet and an extra Brainwriting Worksheet with Random Words, three worksheets per person

- Handout 11–2: Metaphorical Thinking

- Handout 11–4: Cracking Questions

- Handout 11–8: Think 360

- Handout 11–9: Quadrant Collaboration

- Handout 11–14: Dot Voting with a Difference

- One Innovation Training Initial Course Evaluation with workshop title and date completed for each person (Training Instrument 5–1)

- One Innovation Training Bounce-Back Questionnaire with workshop title and date completed for each person (Training Instrument 5–2)

Using the CD

Some materials for this training session are provided in this workbook and as electronic files on the accompanying CD. To access the electronic files, insert the CD and click on the appropriate Adobe .pdf document. Further directions and help locating and using the files can be found in the appendix, "Using the Compact Disc."

Figure 8–1
Creativity Made Simple Workshop Map

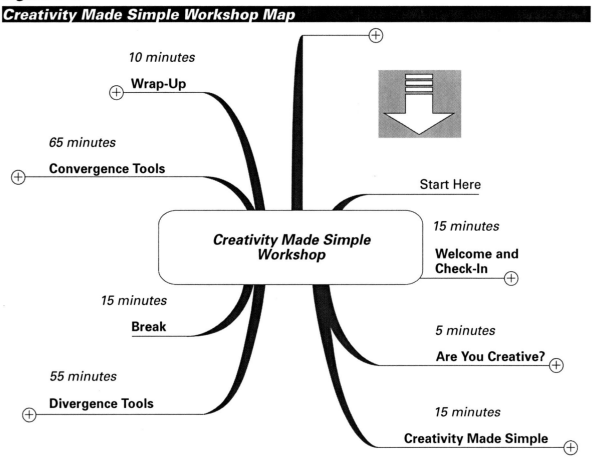

Three-Hour Creativity Made Simple Workshop Sample Agenda

Figure 8–1 is a condensed black-and-white version of the full-color map for this workshop (Figure 8–2.pdf on the CD).

8:30 a.m.   Room Set-Up

Make sure everything is in place and working and all handouts are available for each participant.

Prepare a summary agenda on an easel sheet using the agenda map as a guide.

Have name tags and sheets of colored dots (red, green, blue, yellow) at the tables where groups of four or five people will sit.

Scatter the random magazine images on a table at the back of the room (or on the floor if necessary). If you have a large group, you may need to use two tables so that people have easy access to the images.

9:00   Welcome and Check-In (15 minutes)

Welcome participants to the program, introduce yourself, and provide background about the purpose of the program. If people do not already know each other, allow time for a quick introduction process of name, organization, location, and description of what they do to exercise their personal creativity.

Review the agenda.

Learning Activity 10–1: What's Your Thinking Style? Give each participant a copy of Handout 11–1 and have him or her determine which responses best describes his or her thinking style. Direct each participant to put a dot of the color that corresponds to that style on his or her name tag. Some people will want more than one dot; encourage them to choose one or, at the most, two.

9:15   Are You Creative? (5 minutes)

Review and facilitate Learning Activity 10–10: Are You Creative? This activity helps everyone realize that creativity is an innate trait of all people and understand the confusion between "big-C" Creativity and "little-c" creativity. The activity uses a simple story to illustrate the difference.

9:20   Creativity Made Simple (15 minutes)

Review Handout 11–13: Creativity Made Simple: SWAMI SOARS!, which gives participants a general overview of creativity, its two phases (divergence and convergence), the one critical rule for separating the two phases, a breakdown of the processes of divergence and convergence, and one simple tool for each process.

Briefly explain each of the five processes of divergence and convergence.

Explain the importance of articulating a powerful challenge to focus thinking on the right issue. Invite the group to work on the following challenge: *How might we generate great ideas in our organization?*

Write the challenge on an easel sheet that will remain in view at all times. Explain that this is a challenge that is relevant to the focus of the workshop and the ideas developed could be useful to the organization. If participants accept this challenge, explain that they will be using a complete process to generate and evaluate ideas, and that the final concept(s) selected and the names of the workshop attendees will be forwarded to management.

Give each person a copy of Handout 11–6: Better Brainstorming Guidelines. Let people take turns reading the guidelines out loud until they have all been read.

9:35   Divergence Tools (55 minutes overall)

Explain that the group is going to go through the creativity process focused on the challenge, using five different idea-stimulation tools to generate a large quantity of ideas.

Facilitate Learning Activity 10–3: Cracking Questions (8 minutes). This activity helps participants generate questions that will open their minds to new possibilities.

9:45   Facilitate Learning Activity 10–5: BrainwritingPlus (15 minutes).

Use the Brainwriting Worksheet with Random Words. Keep the sheets moving among people and even among tables to keep the energy flowing.

10:00   Future Stories (10 minutes)

Pick up all the BrainwritingPlus worksheets and put any that are full in a separate stack from those that still have open squares. Make sure each table has at least one empty brainwriting sheet for each person, plus whatever partially filled worksheets that can be apportioned to each table.

Begin a tally of completed sheets on an easel pad so that you can have a total count at the end of the session. There are 15 idea boxes on each worksheet. While groups are working, the completed sheets can be cut apart so that individual ideas can be put into the Idea Basket.

When the brainwriting sheets have been picked up, have the group start work on stories using the following scene: *Assume that it's two years in the future and your challenge—getting your organization to create great ideas—has succeeded beyond expectations. What headlines can you imagine being written about the work your organization has done? What is the story behind the headline? What had to happen to make this newsworthy event a reality?*

Have the team at each table write 10 different headlines and then pick one headline and develop the story that goes with it. Give them about six minutes for this work and then have them stop and return to the brainwriting sheets with any ideas that might have been sparked by these stories.

10:10   Random Images (10 minutes)

Pick up any completed brainwriting sheets and make sure that empty forms for each person are on the tables. Add the number of completed worksheets to your tally. While groups are working, the completed sheets can be cut apart and individual ideas put into the Idea Basket.

Have people go to the table where you scattered images from magazines and tell them to pick three or four images each. Tell them not to spend a lot of time selecting images. When they return to their tables they should use the images to spark new ideas that they will then put on the brainwriting forms. Remind people to build on ideas that are already on the forms.

10:20   Metaphorical Thinking (5 minutes)

Pick up completed brainwriting worksheets and make sure there's a clean worksheet for each person at the table. Add the number of completed worksheets to your tally. While groups are working, the completed sheets can be cut apart and individual ideas put into the Idea Basket.

Explain that metaphorical thinking is the process of thinking about one thing by comparing it with something else. Use an example from the room you're working in. For instance, the floor: it is a foundation for the walls, is strong, and is covered with soft material to make it warmer and more attractive. How do those qualities apply to the challenge of generating great ideas? For example, if everyone felt like their ideas were the *foundation* of the organization, they would be more interested in contributing them. People generating and sharing a lot of new ideas make the organization *strong*. Maybe there is an "idea gym" where people can work out new ideas and make them stronger. Maybe we could *carpet* the idea submission process to make it more appealing. Work through another example by picking an object and having the group identify the qualities and then apply those qualities to the challenge.

Give every attendee Handout 11–2 and tell them that it will help them use this tool when they want to generate ideas on other challenges. They will not need it for this exercise.

Have everyone put their random images in the center of the table. Ask that each person select a new image. They should examine the image and think about the qualities of the people, objects, or actions depicted. They should apply these qualities to the challenge to see what new ideas they stimulate. These ideas should be added to the worksheets.

Remind participants to build on the ideas of others. If they have enough time, they should choose another metaphor and repeat the process.

While the group is generating ideas on this last round, pick up sheets as they are completed. Add the number of completed worksheets to your tally. Call time and have the people at each table determine the number of ideas they have on their sheets. Add those to your tally to get a total number of ideas generated.

10:25   Divergence Debriefing (5 minutes)

Debrief the divergence tools by asking people if they were surprised by the number of ideas generated. Ask them which tools worked for them and ask for any insights they had during the process. Most people find some tools more useful than others. Explain that this is fine and relates both to their thinking styles and to the particular situation.

10:30   Break (15 minutes)

Tell people what time to return and ask for their cooperation in being back on time.

While the group is on break, cut the remaining idea sheets apart and put the pieces in the Idea Basket. If you have a lot of sheets to cut apart, enlist the help of some of the attendees or continue cutting as the groups work through the three color-sorting process that follow the break

Put three sheets of construction paper (one each of red, yellow, and green) on each table.

10:45   Convergence Tools (65 minutes overall)

Explain to the group that you are now going to work with the ideas that were developed in the Divergence session. Divide the ideas that have been cut apart among the tables, placing them in the center of each table.

Criteria Development (5 minutes)

Have the participants at each table come up with three criteria for evaluating the ideas, for example, cost, time, fit with culture, idea yield, and so forth. When the groups have discussed criteria, capture them on an easel sheet. You will be working with criteria later so this can be a pretty rough first cut.

10:50   Three-Color Sort (10 minutes)

Explain that this is one way of identifying the best ideas generated. Keeping in mind the criteria developed at each table, the ideas should be divided into three color groups:

1. Red—doesn't fit criteria

2. Green—fits criteria

3. Yellow—doesn't seem to fit criteria but has something about it that's interesting.

The colored construction sheets should be laid flat on the table with some space between them. Each person then takes some of the ideas and sorts them onto the appropriate color. Because this is supposed to be a fast process, encourage people to do it silently and not to worry too much about where the ideas wind up. The process continues until the ideas are all sorted or until time is up for this process. If you run out of time, remind participants that you still have all the ideas and anyone who wants to take them and continue to process them may do so after the workshop.

11:00   Quadrant Collaboration (15 minutes)

At each table place a sheet of easel paper labeled "Green Ideas" and have groups tape their green ideas on that sheet (if more sheets are needed, supply them.) Tape the sheet(s) to the wall close to each table. Now distribute sheets labeled "Yellow Ideas." Ask participants to tape their yellow ideas to it and put that sheet on a wall at the back or front of the room. Yellow Idea sheets from all of the tables should be grouped together.

Review Learning Activity 10–7: Quadrant Collaboration; using only Handout 11–6 at this time.

Tool 8–1

Quadrant Chart Example

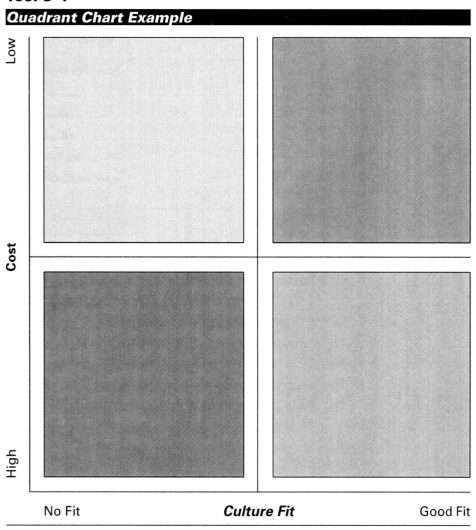

Place a sheet of easel paper at each table and have participants construct a quadrant chart using any two criteria from the list they created previously. Demonstrate this at the easel using the criteria of "cost" and "fit with culture" (see Tool 8–1). Remind them that they should pick their own two criteria...the ones they think are most important.

People at each table will then take the ideas from their "Green Ideas" sheet and determine where the ideas fit on the quadrant chart. This should be done quickly without a lot of discussion. Remind them that they're not eliminating ideas, just creating some sense of order.

Demonstrate the placement of ideas on your quadrant chart (which should look similar to Tool 8–1), using the appropriate criteria on the axes.

While the groups are working on their quadrant charts, pick up all the "red ideas" (those that didn't fit the criteria) and put them in the manila envelope marked "Red Ideas." This can be given to anyone who wants to pursue this project for further development or implementation. It lets people know that although they were not judged as appropriate for the existing situation, ideas are *not* being thrown away.

11:15   Learning Activity 10–6: Think 360 (10 minutes)

Review this learning activity and adapt it to this session. Have participants at each table pick one idea from their quadrant chart that they would like to explore further. Again, it doesn't matter which idea they choose; this is simply an opportunity to experience the process. Work through the Think 360 process focusing on that particular idea, making any adjustments or improvements that occur during the exercise. If a fatal flaw is found in the idea, participants should select another idea and repeat the process.

After eight minutes, have them rewrite the concept using as much detail as possible. Remind them that they are developing a concept to submit to the management of their organization.

11:25   Bullet Proofing (5 minutes)

If you thought someone might shoot at you, you'd probably want to wear a bullet-proof vest. This technique asks each group to think about all the things that might go wrong when presenting and implementing their ideas. Where are the potential failure points? Who might say "no"? What unforeseen disasters might strike? When they've identified the "bullets," they can spend some time protecting themselves...or they may decide that being hit by bullets is so unlikely that there's no point in worrying about protection. Make notes of possible problems. In a real project, some of these might require extensive rethinking and brainstorming.

For this activity, participants are only going to identify potential problems with the idea—not actually devise protection. Rewrite the concept incorporating any new thoughts. (Remind them to make it legible because other people will be reading it.)

11:30   Dot Voting with a Difference (10 minutes)

Review Handout 11–14: Dot Voting with a Difference. Have each team post its concept in a place where everyone can see it. Remind people to review the criteria list. Give each of them two red dots with which to vote. They can vote for two concepts or vote twice for one.

Ask someone from each table to explain the group's concept and, after all the concepts have been presented, ask participants to vote. As people are voting and moving from one idea to another, building ideas often come up, so reserve a few minutes during which people can share any ideas that were developed during the voting. Someone from each table should be capturing on sticky notes the ideas related to their concept so that they can include them on the concept paper later.

Remind people that in a regular process of development, they would want to look again at all the Yellow Ideas to see if there are any gems there that should be explored further.

11:40   Convergence Debriefing (10 minutes)

Facilitate a discussion about the convergence process. What worked and what didn't? Ask participants if they would like to have the concept papers submitted to management. If they would, have everyone sign their name on one blank sheet of paper that can be attached to the concept development sheet. Ask for volunteers to write up the concepts for submission.

11:50   Wrap-Up (10 minutes)

Ask people to talk at their tables about one thing that they plan to use in their "normal" work. Give them about two minutes for this and then ask people to share generally.

Ask them how they might share what they learned today with their associates.

Ask for any questions and pass out the black-and-white version of the workshop map. Explain that it is an overview of the material covered today to make it easier to share the information with their associates back on the job.

Noon   Close

Distribute the bounce-back questionnaire for the workshop (refer to Training Instrument 5–2) and explain the process that you will use to monitor the effectiveness of what they learned here today.

What to Do Next

- ◆ Prepare for the three-hour creativity session.

- ◆ Compile and review the learning activities, handouts, and materials you will use in your training.

- ◆ Determine the schedule and location for the training classes.

- ◆ Invite participants.

◆ ◆ ◆

The next chapter guides you through a three-hour workshop designed to increase innovation competencies.

Chapter 9

Personal Innovation Competencies— Three-Hour Workshop

What's in This Chapter?

- Description of personal innovation competencies

- Discussion of the PIC Gap Analysis

- Design for a three-hour personal innovation competencies workshop

- Overview map of the workshop

- Detailed sample program agenda

- Instructions for conducting the workshop

People often wonder...

"How can I think more creatively?"

or

"How can I be more innovative?"

Through InnovationNetwork's conferences, workshops, and other activities, we were asked these questions so many times that we created an inventory of competencies—called the Personal Innovation Competencies (PIC)—that people can cultivate to maximize innovation.

The workshop outlined here is designed for anyone who wants to improve her or his own innovation capabilities. Participants may come from teams or functions that demand innovation on a regular basis, or they simply may be interested in innovation and wish to know how to contribute more. The basis for the workshop is a self-assessment that you will help participants navigate. Then you will help them create learning plans for building specific practices or skills. Participants will take away both a greater understanding of ways they can strengthen their innovation muscle and an action plan for doing so.

What Are Personal Innovation Competencies?

There are nine categories of competencies that we've identified as elemental to becoming a master innovator. The PIC Gap Analysis measures several specific behaviors or practices in each of the following categories:

1. Commits to the exploration and development of new possibilities

2. Seeks out and creates new connections between unrelated concepts

3. Commits to the creation of customer value

4. Integrates the specific business strategy with the process of innovation

5. Builds alignment around new possibilities

6. Cultivates genuine relationships

7. Embraces appropriate risk taking

8. Effectively manages innovation projects

9. Learns relentlessly.

Here are brief descriptions of each of the nine categories:

1. **Commits to the exploration and development of new possibilities:** The first competency for innovation involves openness, exploration, and the ability to envision and promote new possibilities. By its very nature innovation seeks a better way. Innovators are like explorers. They push forward into uncharted territory, sometimes just to find out what's there. They open themselves to ideas that are unfamiliar and perhaps disconcerting.

2. **Seeks out and creates new connections between unrelated concepts:** There will always be original ideas generated and new technologies developed, but most money is made on improving existing ideas and finding new combinations of previously unrelated concepts—the essence of creative thinking. The keys to discovering these recombinations include constant scanning of what's going on in the world, using whole-brain thinking, investigating anomalies, and experimenting.

3. **Commits to create customer value:** The focal point of innovation is the customer, whether internal or external. Successful innovators dig deep to understand their customer's or user's most

profound concerns. It is the intersection of customer needs and concerns with your organization's strategy and goals that allows for the solutions that customers value.

4. **Integrates specific business focus with the process of innovation:** Great innovators are also good businesspeople. They keep pace with their industries and are aware of what others are doing. They are also masters of the tools, methodologies, and practices that represent their industries' standards, and they are skillful at the process of innovation. Part of innovation is the constant sharpening of business acumen and expertise in one's own field. The other part is mastery of the practices and tools of innovation, per se.

5. **Builds alignment around new possibilities:** Innovation starts with an idea, and ideas need champions to nurture and promote them. Competent innovators understand stakeholder concerns and can connect the dots between vision and the ideas that will enable the vision. They paint compelling pictures of the future, embrace the ideas of others, and facilitate communication and alignment around ideas and actions.

6. **Cultivates genuine relationships:** Innovation requires trust and collaboration because no idea can flourish without a team effort. To be an effective collaborator, one must honor and respect the opinions of others, and be sincere, reliable, and compassionately honest. Building productive relationships with colleagues is hard work, but it is the foundation for tremendous success and fulfillment.

7. **Embraces appropriate risk taking:** Knowing the difference between a calculated risk and simply risky business is paramount in innovation. Understanding what risk means to self, team, and organization is the first step. Identifying risk factors, being able to track them, and communicating openly about them makes for solid risk management.

8. **Effectively manages innovation projects:** Projects often must adjust over time with the changing business and economic climate. By definition, innovative projects should be flexible and focused on the creation of value. Effective innovators pay close attention to managing promises, juggling priorities, making decisions, and timing for actions. They leverage tools, processes, and methodologies in a conscious fashion to reach intended results.

9. **Learns relentlessly.** Master innovators are curious. Their endless searches for what's, how's, and why's fuel new ideas and vast possibilities. Successful innovation often requires much experimentation and leaves many failures in its wake. Innovators who seek feedback, examine the reasons behind success or failure, and challenge their own assumptions will find themselves constantly propelled forward.

Personal Innovation Competencies (PIC) Gap Analysis

To improve any capabilities it is important to establish a baseline of the current state and to identify specific targets for improvement. The PIC Gap Analysis provides a simple self-assessment format that speaks both to today's state and to desired improvement. With the completed gap analysis, you can help a person create his or her learning plan to build the skills and practices for innovation using the PIC Personal Action Worksheet. The PIC Gap Analysis (Handout 11–16) and the PIC Personal Action Worksheet (Handout 11–17) are available both in the book and on the CD.

In the PIC Gap Analysis, there are nine categories containing three to five specific items for which participants will assess themselves. They will use the following ratings:

- **Unknowing:** This is new thinking to me.

- **Novice:** I understand and practice this behavior about 10 percent of the time.

- **Advanced Beginner:** I'm getting the hang of it and practice this behavior 10–25 percent of the time.

- **Competent:** I really get it and demonstrate this behavior 25–50 percent of the time.

- **Proficient:** I model this behavior more than 50 percent of the time and am beginning to mentor others.

- **Master:** I embody this behavior more than 90 percent of the time and am evolving higher standards.

To see how these ratings are arranged, see the PIC Gap Analysis (Handout 11–16).

For each item, participants mark an "A" in the column that indicates their current understanding or practices and a "B" in the column that indicates the level they wish to achieve in the future. There are 38 line items on the assessment—but don't be alarmed! You will be helping each workshop participant focus on the two or three items that they really want to improve in the short term.

Training Objectives

The objectives of the Personal Innovation Competencies (PIC) Workshop are to

- familiarize participants with individual competencies that are important to innovation

- assess participants' current abilities and practices related to key innovation competencies

- determine a small set of practices that participants wish to build or improve on

- teach participants ways to build competencies

- help participants create an action-learning plan to address those competencies they wish to build.

Target Audience

This workshop is appropriate for anyone in the organization who wishes to increase his or her individual capabilities to innovate or contribute to innovation. Ideal group sizes for these exercises are a minimum of nine participants and can easily accommodate up to 45. If you are planning for between nine and 27 participants, allow an extra 20 to 40 minutes overall (see the variables described below in the sample agenda). Advise participants in advance of any variation in predicted time commitment.

Materials

For the facilitator:

- Four or five poster-sized copies of the InnovationDNA graphic for the walls

- Eight to 10 stimulating quotes or inspirational photos mounted on colored paper for the walls

- Small toys; avoid toys that make noise

- Small dish of candies for each table

For the participants:

- One PIC Gap Analysis for each person (Handout 11–16)

- One PIC Discussion Guide for up to nine groups (Handout 11–18)

- One copy of the Personal Innovation Competencies for each person (Handout 11–19)

- One PIC Personal Action Worksheet for each person (Handout 11–17)

- One 3x5-inch pad of sticky notes for each person

- One black, medium-point marking pen per person

- Flipchart easel, paper, and three colored markers per group

- One Innovation Training Initial Course Evaluation with workshop title and date completed for each person (Training Instrument 5–1)

- One Innovation Training Bounce-Back Questionnaire with workshop title and date completed for each person (Training Instrument 5–2)

Room Logistics

Make sure the room is organized, neat, and inviting. Hang poster-sized copies of the InnovationDNA graphic on the wall, as well as stimulating quotes and colorful photos and artwork.

Set up tables so groups of three to five people can work together. Scatter some small toys on the tables.

Place dishes of candy on the tables and provide refreshments for break.

Three-Hour Personal Innovation Competencies Workshop Sample Agenda

Figure 9–1 is a condensed black-and-white version of the full-color map for this workshop (Figure 9–2.pdf on the CD).

Figure 9–1

Personal Innovation Competencies Workshop Map

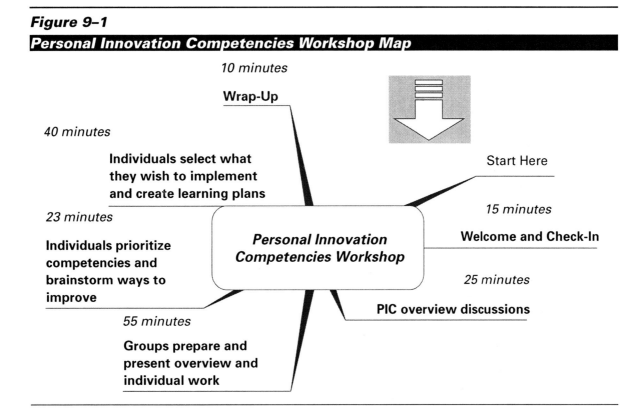

In this workshop participants will become familiar with nine categories of individual competencies that affect innovation. A self-assessment tool is used to identify both the current and desired states of those competencies. Participants then create a learning plan focused on building a manageable number of specific skills or practices.

8:00 a.m.   Room Preparation (30 minutes)

To determine your discussion format—the way you form discussion groups for the PIC overviews—consider the following factors: There are nine PIC categories to discuss. The ideal arrangement would be to have nine groups of three to five participants each so that all of the categories are covered in one round of discussion. If you have fewer than 27 participants, determine if the nine categories can be covered more adequately in two or in three rounds. For example, with 12 participants three groups of four would go through three rounds of discussions to cover the nine categories. There should be no more than five people at a table.

Arrange the tables and chairs according to the discussion group format you choose.

At each participant's seat, place a PIC Gap Analysis (but not the PIC Personal Action Worksheet), a pad of sticky notes, and a marking pen.

8:30   Welcome and Introduction (3 minutes)

Welcome participants.

Explain the objectives of the workshop:

- to become familiar with individual competencies that are important to innovation

- to assess current levels of competency

- to identify a small set of practices to build or improve on

- to learn about ways to build those competencies

- to create an action plan to do so.

8:33   Check-In (12 minutes)

Ask everyone to think of their key expectation for today's workshop. If your class is 12 or fewer you can have each person, in turn, introduce herself or himself and state that key expectation. Write the expectations on the flipchart. If your class is larger than 12, give each group of participants five minutes to check in with the others at their table, and then ask a person at each table report one or two expectations that are common to the group. Note those on a flipchart.

Address any expectations that will likely not be met in the workshop.

8:45   Launch the PIC overview discussions (30 minutes overall).

Using a random method (such as counting off), assemble participants into groups of at least three people—refer to your predetermined discussion format and groups.

Randomly distribute the PIC Discussion Guide (Handout 11–18), one to each group. (If multiple discussion rounds, you will distribute remaining discussion guides when appropriate.)

Explain the activity as follows:

"In this activity your groups will be learning about and discussing one or more categories of Personal Innovation Competencies.

"Each group has been assigned a different set of competencies, and you will have a Discussion Guide for each set.

"You will have 20 minutes to read through the category overview and discuss the questions in the guide. If you don't finish all the questions, that's okay; it's the quality of your discussion that matters.

"Be sure to take notes of the key points in your discussion on either the sticky notes or the flipchart paper. I suggest you take turns being scribe.

"After your discussions you will have five minutes to organize a two- to three-minute presentation to the larger group, focusing on the definition of the category and the key points of your discussion.

"After each presentation, everyone will complete the section for that category on the PIC Gap Analysis. *[Hold up a copy of the PIC Gap Analysis for visual reference.]*

"Are there any questions?"

8:50   Repeat that participants will have 20 minutes and let them begin.

Give a time update when 13 minutes have passed.

9:10   Announce that discussion time is over and they have five minutes to organize their two- to three-minute presentations for the large group.

9:15   Team Presentations (about 50 minutes)

Before you begin the presentations, remind participants that they will complete the PIC Gap Analysis by category following the presentations.

The presentations may be made in any order.

After each presentation have participants turn to the respective category on the Gap Analysis and complete their self-assessment of that section (2 minutes each).

Keep this process moving as quickly as participants can handle.

(If groups are working on multiple categories, allow 18 minutes for subsequent discussion rounds. Take the 15 minute break after discussion round 2.)

10: 05   Break (15 minutes)

Ask those who have not completed their PIC Gap Analysis to do so during the break.

Place sets of the Personal Innovation Competencies and PIC Personal Action Worksheets at participants' places.

10:20   Selecting Competencies to Build (7 minutes overall)

Ask participants to review their PIC Gap Analysis self-assessments, using Handout 11–19 as reference for definitions or clarifications (4 minutes).

Ask them to select two or three competencies they would like to build on and write them in the appropriate blanks on the PIC Personal Action Worksheet (3 minutes).

10: 27   Brainstorming Ways to Build Competencies and Selecting Ideas to Implement (24 minutes overall)

Ask participants to prioritize the competencies they chose to build (2 minutes).

Have them form groups by their highest-priority competency category (2 minutes).

Ask participants to share with each other the specific competencies they chose and why (5–10 minutes, depending on the number of groups).

Ask them to brainstorm together *specific* ideas on how to build competencies in this category. They can use the general ideas listed on Handout 11–19 as a starting point, but their task is to generate specific, actionable ideas that they can personally implement. For example, if the general idea is to "read major business publications," a specific idea for that is to "subscribe to and regularly read the *Harvard Business Review*." Ask them to write their ideas on sticky notes, one idea per sheet (10 minutes).

10:51   Selecting Ideas to Implement (4 minutes)

Instruct each participant to choose one to three ideas they could implement (2 minutes).

Have them write those ideas in the appropriate boxes on their PIC Personal Action Worksheets (2 minutes).

10:55   Brainstorming and Selecting Ideas for Their Second- and Third-Priority Competencies (35 minutes overall)

Have everyone now regroup on the basis of their second-priority competency and repeat the brainstorming and the selection process their second priority category (16–17 minutes).

If time allows, have participants regroup for their third-priority competency and repeat the process. If time does not allow, have them work individually for a few minutes on their third priority or assign it as postsession work.

11: 30   Completing Their Learning Plans (9 minutes)

Begin by explaining that everyone should now have found a number of ideas they'd like to implement and that it is time to commit to those very few ideas that they truly might y take action on.

Ask them to highlight or otherwise mark two or three ideas they are willing to commit to action (2 minutes).

Ask them to think of a way to measure progress for each idea and to write those ways in the metric columns (2 minutes).

Ask them to create at least their Month 1 goals, if not all three goals, for each idea (2 minutes).

Note that instructions are also provided on the worksheets.

Give them two to three more minutes to complete their worksheets.

Distribute copies of the Initial Course Evaluations and the Bounce-Back.

11:40   Closing comments and evaluations (10 minutes)

Congratulate participants on their learning plans and thank them for their enthusiasm.

Note any housekeeping issues.

Have participants complete and hand in the Innovation Training Initial Course Evaluation.

Explain the Bounce-Back and Notice of Completion system, pointing out that the course is not truly complete until its value on the job can be determined. Tell them you will email the Bounce-Back to them in 7 to 10 days. When they respond, you will send the Notice of Completion and a Certificate of Completion to their managers or supervisors. **Ask for commitment (by show of hands) to respond to the Bounce-Back when you email it to them.**

11:50   Check-Out and Adjournment (10 minutes)

If possible in the large group, ask everyone to quickly share one personal strength they already have that contributes to innovation in the organization. Set a quick pace by starting with a very brief sentence about *your* strength.

Thank each participant after their share—we hope the entire group will catch on to this practice.

What to Do Next

- ◆ Prepare for the three-hour Personal Innovation Competencies session.

- ◆ Compile the handouts and forms for the training session.

- ◆ Determine schedule and room logistics for classes.

- ◆ Invite participants.

- ◆ Determine class size, discussion format, and advise participants of workshop time commitment.

◆ ◆ ◆

In the following chapter, you will find leaning activities that support the InnovationDNA, Innovation Comes Alive!, and Creativity Made Simple workshops.

This is the conclusion of our narrative to you. Good luck in your efforts to spur innovation in your organization. We hope you will find it fun and rewarding...and that you won't be afraid to express your creativity!

Learning Activities

- ◆ Notes on using the accompanying CD

- ◆ Tips for trainers

- ◆ Eleven learning activities

- ◆ Detailed instructions for using the learning activities

This chapter includes all of the learning activities that are used in the designs for the training sessions presented in chapters 6 through 9. Each learning activity includes the following information:

- ◆ Target audience

- ◆ Goals and objectives

- ◆ Materials

- ◆ Time

- ◆ Instructions

- ◆ Debriefing

Using the Accompanying CD

You will find the handouts, slides, and other materials referred to in this chapter on the CD that accompanies this workbook. To access those files, insert the CD and click on the file name you want.

To print the materials for your training session, follow these simple steps: Insert the CD and click on the appropriate .pdf file name to open it in Adobe Acrobat software. Print the pages of the document(s) needed for your training session. Most of the .pdf files are black-and-white documents; a few are presented in color to make them more visually comprehensible.

The PowerPoint slide presentations referred to in the learning activities are available on the CD. You can use the entire presentation or choose individual slides to suit your customized content by opening the presentation, saving the file under a different name, and deleting the slides you do not want to use. The following PowerPoint presentations are provided on the CD:

+ *InnovationDNA.ppt*

+ *Metaphorical Thinking.ppt*

+ *Springboard Stories.ppt*

For additional instructions on using the CD, see the appendix, "Using the Compact Disc," at the end of the workbook.

Tips for Trainers

Before using these learning activities in your training sessions, be sure to review chapters 1 through 5 for background on how this training program was developed. As in all training, adding your personal touch by sharing your own stories will make the content come alive. Feel free to describe your experiences whenever those might be helpful. Customizing the learning activities with examples from your organization will also add value to the program.

Be flexible. The timeframes for many of these activities can be changed according to your own goals and needs. You may find that you cover key concepts in the course of discussion and that you no longer need to include certain activities or content materials. Or you may find that additional discussion is needed to clarify certain concepts. Stay with the participants . . . it's more important that they learn some things well than that they are force-marched through a preconceived agenda.

Debriefing workshop activities is an extremely important part of the learning process. Whenever possible, add a few minutes to the quoted time to ask standard questions such as these: How could you use this activity in your work? What insights did you have? Did anything surprise you?

Time for many of the activities is given as a range—for example: 15–25 minutes. The smaller number is suggested as a minimum and the larger number gives you more time for discussion and debriefing. Small groups of fewer than 10 participants generally can complete the activity in the smaller amount of time. Larger groups will need more time to have a complete discussion. Stay tuned in with the participants.

Learning Activity 10–1: Innovation Openers

The eight variants in this activity are brief energizers to help people explore different aspects of innovation.

TARGET AUDIENCE

The target audience for this activity is anyone who wants to have a deeper understanding of innovation.

GOALS AND OBJECTIVES

The goals and objectives for this learning activity are to

- ◆ break the ice and get people talking in small groups

- ◆ provide opportunities for participants to think about experiences of innovation

- ◆ stimulate thought about different aspects of innovation.

MATERIALS

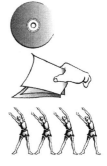

Nametags are needed for all of the eight possible activities described here. Additional materials are needed for four of the variants:

- ◆ Handout 11–1: What's Your Thinking Style? (Learning Activity 10–1A)

- ◆ Colored dots (red, green, yellow, and blue), enough for each participant (Learning Activity 10–1A)

- ◆ Large quantity of 4x4-inch sticky notes (Learning Activity 10–1B)

- ◆ Handout 11–2: Metaphorical Thinking (Learning Activity 10–1D)

- ◆ 4x6-inch sticky notes in two colors (yellow and green), one note of each color for every participant (Learning Activity 10–1H)

- ◆ *Metaphorical Thinking.ppt*

TIME

- ◆ 10 minutes for each variant

INSTRUCTIONS

Learning Activity 10–1A: What's Your Thinking Style?

1. Explain that there are many different ways of thinking and that it's important to have a diversity of thinking styles when we're trying to generate ideas or implement new projects. Understanding the different thinking styles helps us work together more effectively.

2. Emphasize that each person is capable of using all thinking styles but generally is energized by only one style.

3. Distribute Handout 11–1: What's Your Thinking Style? Read through the handout so that you are thoroughly familiar with the process and can guide the participants through the activity. The handout is primarily a resource and reminder for the participants after they leave the workshop. Ask participants to answer both of the questions and then put an X by the appropriate answer. This will show each person whether he or she is a Red (Teaching), Green (Organizing), Yellow (Exploring), or Blue (Problem-Solving) thinker, as described in the handout. When each participant has decided which quadrant best describes him or her, each should place the appropriate colored dot on his or her nametag.

4. Designate each corner of the room a specific color and have people go to the corners that represent their preferred thinking styles.

5. Have them look around the room to see which colors, if any, predominate. Ask them how it could help them if they better understood thinking styles.

Learning Activity 10–1B: Wouldn't It Be Great If. . . ?

1. Explain that the question "Wouldn't it be great if. . . ? " is an excellent means of clarifying vision, and that it can be used at the beginning of any project.

2. Have the group develop a concept of something they would like to improve. You can either have them brainstorm some improvement areas for a minute or so, or have three or four concepts prepared that they can vote on. Typical concepts include the following: improve communication, reduce costs, enhance customer satisfaction, process [*x*] faster, and so on.

3. When participants have selected the area of improvement that they are willing to think about for a few minutes, have them write on sticky notes 10 "Wouldn't it be great if. . . ? " ideas, one per sticky note. Suggest a few far-fetched ideas to get them loosened up: "Wouldn't it be great if we instantly knew everything that was going on around here? . . . if we could make meetings shorter and more effective? . . . if we never got copied on e-mails that we weren't interested in?"

4. Give people three or four minutes to write their ideas. Then ask them to read them aloud, one at a time. Tell the rest of the group to listen for themes or for possibilities that particularly interest them. Explain that participants in a real brainstorming session would take one or two of the most exciting possibilities and begin to suggest ways to make them happen.

5. Give people a couple of minutes to discuss the benefits of this activity.

Learning Activity 10–1C: Customer Archetype Story

1. Break the group into teams of three or four people.

2. Explain that each team is to make up a story about a typical customer (internal or external). They should create a name for this customer and begin describing the customer and situation: where he lives, what her family life is like, what he looks like, what she does for a living, how old he is, how she uses your product or service, what it means to him, how she feels about it, what he wishes it would do that it doesn't, how she describes it to her friends.

3. Give the teams about five minutes to make up their stories and then spend the remainder of the time letting them share their stories with the whole group.

Learning Activity 10–1D: Innovation Here Is Like . . .

Metaphors are powerful thinking tools. This activity gives people a chance to compare something they have some sense of with a totally unrelated object. What they will find is that the concept and the object are not as unrelated as they initially thought, and the process of comparing the two will reveal new insights.

1. Read Handout 11–2: Metaphorical Thinking and give participants an overview of what metaphors are and how they can be important in stimulating new ideas and connections.

2. Ask them to think about innovation in their organization and to pick an image as a metaphor. Give them an example from something in the room; for instance, innovation is like that lamp because when it's on there's light in the room and we can all see better, and because it's easy for anyone to turn it off.

3. Give people a few minutes to pick a metaphor and think about how it relates to innovation in their organization. Then have people talk at their tables about the metaphors they chose and why.

4. If there is time, ask individuals to share a few thoughts with the large group.

5. Give each participant a copy of Handout 11–2: Metaphorical Thinking as a resource for future use.

6. *Optional:* You can also use the Metaphorical Thinking slide to provide people with metaphors from objects outside the room.

Learning Activity 10–1E: Innovation Story

1. Explain that innovation is not a completely new thing...almost everyone has been involved with innovation before, whether in a new project at work or at home. Remind them of the definition of innovation: *people creating value by implementing new ideas.*

2. Ask participants to think of a time in their professional or personal lives when they were involved in innovation. Have them pair up with another person and tell that person about the experience. Tell them to share not only what happened but also how they felt about the experience. Give the pairs about six minutes to tell their stories and prompt them at the halfway point so that they can change storytellers.

3. Spend the rest of the time letting people share their stories with the large group. Often you will see themes emerging from these stories. You might want to capture these themes on a sheet of flipchart paper or just take notes and then highlight them at the end of the discussion.

Learning Activity 10–1F: Dream Team

1. Before the workshop, identify a possible project that would interest the participants of the workshop. It should be general enough to be interesting and understandable to everyone, but specific enough to

stimulate their thinking. For example, "improve communication" is general enough to be understood by everyone, but it is also very broad and vague. A better choice might be "create better communication between accounting and marketing."

2. Ask people to form groups of three or four.

3. Tell the participants that they have a huge project ahead of them—one that will have a lot of visibility throughout the organization and that may positively or negatively affect their careers. Briefly explain the project. Tell them that their team will figure out what should be done and then implement it. Their immediate task is to decide who should be on the project team, identifying them not by name but by skill, experience, perspective, or any other quality they think would be important to the team. Note that they are not limited to current employees of the organization; rather, they can pick from the world at large. Reiterate that they are choosing by the qualities they're looking for rather than by name. Tell them that the project team can have no more than 10 members.

4. Give groups six minutes to come up with their dream teams.

5. Spend the rest of the time having each group describe an ideal team and explain why certain qualities were important.

6. If the workshop has a large number of participants, pair groups and have them describe their team selections to one another.

7. Reserve a few minutes to spend highlighting qualities that seem to be common to various teams. Emphasize the importance of diversity in thinking styles, skills, perspectives, experiences, and so on. If it hasn't come out in the discussion, bring up the importance of including people who are passionate and committed to the success of the project.

Learning Activity 10–1G: Best Failure Story

1. Explain to participants that, by definition, innovation is doing something new, something that has never been done before. Therefore it might fail. Tolerating failure and learning from it are critical ingredients in the innovation mix.

2. Ask participants to form pairs. Have each person think of a failure she or he has experienced in the past, either professional or personal.

3. Ask individuals to share their failure stories with their partners. Have them explain what they learned from their failures and how the failures affected their lives. Have them describe how the world around them responded to the failures? Spend about five minutes on the stories and prompt people at the halfway point so that they can change storytellers.

4. Spend the rest of the time discussing what lessons were learned through the failures, and what insights were gained from the stories?

5. Ask what makes a "smart failure."

Learning Activity 10–1H: Learning and Teaching Offers

1. Pass out yellow and green sticky notes, one of each color to every participant.

2. Explain that learning is not limited to the classroom and that everyone is a learner and a teacher. Have each participant think of one thing he or she would like to learn, either professionally or personally, and write that item on the yellow sticky note.

3. Then ask each one to think of something she or he could teach someone else. This might be as simple as how to use the fax machine or a certain software or it could be as complex as how to remodel a basement. Instruct them to write this on the green sticky note and then to put their names on both stickies.

4. Select a place on the wall where all the yellow "learning" stickies will be posted and a separate place for all the green "teaching" stickies. Tape two large pieces of paper to the wall in those places.

5. Ask people to read their stickies aloud as "I would like to learn how to…." and "I would be willing to teach….." When they've read them, they should put the stickies on the appropriate sheets of paper.

6. Discuss any matches or trends that appear. Ask people if there were any surprises. Talk about life-long learning.

Learning Activity 10–2: Springboard Stories

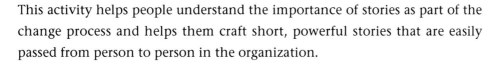

This activity helps people understand the importance of stories as part of the change process and helps them craft short, powerful stories that are easily passed from person to person in the organization.

TARGET AUDIENCE

The target audience for this activity is anyone involved in change processes.

GOALS AND OBJECTIVES

The goals and objectives of this learning activity are to

- ◆ build a better understanding of the Culture element of the InnovationDNA

- ◆ understand the importance of stories, especially in change processes

- ◆ learn the definition of "springboard stories"

- ◆ learn how to recognize good springboard stories, and how to craft and tell them.

MATERIALS

For the instructor:

- ◆ Springboard Stories slide presentation (*Springboard Stories.ppt*)

For the participants:

- ◆ Handout 11–3: Springboard Stories

TIME

- ◆ 15–25 minutes

INSTRUCTIONS

1. Read Handout 11–3 so that you are thoroughly familiar with the process and can tell the World Bank story.

Adapted from Stephen Deming, The Springboard: How Storytelling Ignites Action in Knowledge-Era Organizations, *(Butterworth-Heinemann, 2000).*

2. Pass out a copy of Handout 11–3: Springboard Stories to each participant. This will primarily be a resource for later because you will be guiding participants through the activity.

3. Define springboard stories as stories of change that have been stripped down to their most essential elements so that they can be told quickly and repeated easily.

4. Review the handout with participants and explain the importance of stories in opening up possibilities in people's minds.

5. Present the Springboard Story PowerPoint presentation. Tell the World Bank story. Leave the slide with the seven elements of a springboard story showing.

6. Emphasize that a springboard story must be basically true but that it does not have to include every single detail and nuance because it is being told specifically to plant the possibility of a change in someone's mind. Explain that every detail left in must serve the story and the purpose.

7. Have people pair off and ask each one to think of a story related to change that they can tell their partners. Explain that it takes a while to whittle a story down to its bare essence and that they will not have time to finish crafting the story during this session. Tell them that you want them to find a story and work with a partner to see if it has the elements of a springboard story.

8. Give the pairs several minutes to share their stories, dividing the time equally between the partners. Explain that while one person is telling the story as briefly as possible, the partner should be listening for the elements of a springboard story. When the story has been told, the listening partner should give the teller feedback on how it met the requirements of a springboard story and what was missing. The teller can then look for ways to revise and enhance the story to make it fit the model.

9. For longer programs you may give the pairs more time to craft their stories, or you may choose to have participants switch partners and repeat the process so people hear more stories and gain more experience telling their stories and receiving feedback.

10. Spend the last few minutes discussing the process of finding and telling springboard stories. Ask for a volunteer to tell his or her story. Provide as much positive feedback as possible and gently identify any missing elements.

Learning Activity 10-3: Cracking Questions

This activity gives people a framework to help them understand how to ask better questions.

TARGET AUDIENCE

The target audience for this activity is anyone who wants to be a more effective learner, communicator, leader, or innovator.

GOALS AND OBJECTIVES

The goals and objectives for this activity are to

- build a better understanding of the Challenge element of the InnovationDNA

- emphasize the importance of questions

- provide a theoretical structure to help people ask better questions

- stimulate the development of a repertoire of questions.

MATERIALS

For the instructor:

- Four sheets of flipchart paper taped to the walls, each headed by one of the following phrases printed with the colored markers indicated:

  - Open the Future (red)

  - Reveal New Territory (green)

  - Fill In the Blanks (blue)

  - Find the Heart (purple)

For the participants:

- Handout 11–4: Cracking Questions

- Index cards, at least 20 per table

◆ Markers for all participants

◆ Tape

TIME

◆ 15–25 minutes

INSTRUCTIONS

1. Pass out one copy of Handout 11–4: Cracking Questions to each participant.

2. Explain the importance of questions and tell them that this session will focus on how to develop better questions and how to build a repertoire of great questions.

3. Review the four purposes behind all questions, as they are written on the flipchart sheets hanging on the walls and as described in Handout 11–4.

4. Have people get into small groups of three or four.

5. Ask groups to develop five questions for each of the four question purposes shown on the flipchart sheets. Tell them to write each question legibly with a marker on separate index cards. Give them five minutes to develop the questions.

6. Have each group tape their cards to the appropriate sheets, reading each question aloud to the entire gathering as they do so. Tell them to tape questions that are the same as or similar to ones previously presented on top of the cards already attached. (If there are too many groups for this process to be done in the time allotted, have three groups get together and present their questions.)

7. Direct participants' attention to the 20 questions in Handout 11–4. Ask them to identify questions that they think would be good additions to their question repertoire.

8. If time permits, solicit ideas about an issue of interest to everyone. (If no issues seem energizing to everyone, have them focus on how to get everyone in the organization to have better ideas.) Ask them to develop 10 questions that would help them address this issue more effectively.

9. Discuss the process of thinking about questions in this manner. Ask for insights. Ask for a volunteer to capture all of the questions and send everyone a copy.

10. Discuss potential opportunities for using some of these questions.

Learning Activity 10–4: Breakthrough Generator

This activity is designed to focus thinking on an idea-stimulation process that can be used to develop specific possibilities or powerful challenge statements that can lead to breakthroughs. It is based on specific consumer benefits that have historically resulted in major leaps—dramatic changes in size, speed, convenience, safety, price, distribution, and so on.

TARGET AUDIENCE

The audience for this learning activity includes anyone who needs a deeper understanding of customer benefits or wants to stimulate new ideas or challenge statements that are directly related to important customer benefits.

GOALS AND OBJECTIVES

The goals and objectives for this activity are to

- build a better understanding of the Customer Focus element of the InnovationDNA

- stimulate thinking around the most common customer benefits

- focus thought on customer benefits with the potential to create breakthroughs

- guide participants in the process of developing benefits-based challenge statements.

MATERIALS

For the instructor:

- Handout 11–6: Better Brainstorming Guidelines, posted around the room. If possible, enlarge these to poster size.

- Easel, flipchart paper, and markers

- Sticky notes in three different colors

For the participants:

- Handout 11–5: Breakthrough Generator Matrix

- Handout 11–6: Better Brainstorming Guidelines

- Sticky notes, one pad per person

TIME

◆ 15–25 minutes

INSTRUCTIONS

1. Explain to participants that all customers have certain benefits that are of primary interest to them, even internal customers. Focusing on those benefits stimulates thinking that yields better ideas than the standard "What could we do to make our product *better?*" (How would you define "better" if you *didn't* look at benefits?)

2. Create three flipchart sheets, labeled "Primary Benefits," "Secondary Benefits," and "Actions."

3. Put each of the words and phrases in the matrix depicted in Handout 11–5: Breakthrough Generator Matrix on sticky notes (use a separate color for each category) and post the words on the respective flipchart sheets.

4. Decide whether you want to use this technique to generate challenge statements or actual new ideas. If you want new challenge statements, use option A. If you want to generate new ideas, use option B.

5. Place the Better Brainstorming Guidelines posters on the wall where they can be seen easily and hand out a copy of the guidelines to each participant. Give each person a copy of Handout 11–5: Breakthrough Generator.

6. Explain that breakthrough products and services almost always involve significant improvements in customer benefits related to the benefits listed on the flipchart sheet labeled "Primary Benefits." Focusing on benefits can suggest actual new possibilities, but it can also suggest challenge statements that could stimulate real breakthroughs.

7. Explain that secondary benefits can lead to breakthroughs but more often lead to moderate improvements. (One example is cell phones. The convenience of having your phone with you at all times led to a breakthrough. A new feature of cell phones is the ability to take pictures—that adds some excitement and flexibility but will probably not be a breakthrough in the same sense as the cell phone itself. Another feature is the customizable cell phone faceplate. It's definitely a sec-

ondary benefit that may add revenue and customer satisfaction but will not be a breakthrough that creates major new revenue sources.)

8. Explain to participants that combining primary benefits with secondary benefits and some specific actions stimulates new thinking and powerful new ideas.

9. *Option A, challenge statements:* Have the group think of an issue that is important to them or use internal communication as a topic. If communication is the topic, work through two examples using words chosen somewhat at random from the matrix, such as the following:

   a. **speed/social connection/rearrange**—*Challenge statement:* "How might we increase the speed of communication by rearranging the existing network of social connections?"

   b. **fun/stories/individualize**—*Challenge statement:* "How might we make it fun for individuals to share their stories of lessons learned?"

   Now have the group choose matrix possibilities at random and then use them to develop challenge questions to fit the topic you have chosen. Don't worry about whether they are great questions. Try to get at least five more challenge questions in a few minutes.

10. *Option B, stimulate new ideas:* Decide on a specific challenge statement, such as "How might we improve communication in our organization?" or "How might we stimulate new ideas in our organization?" Make sure each participant has a copy of Handout 11–6: Better Brainstorming Guidelines. Explain that research has shown that simply reading the guidelines to a brainstorming session improves the number and quality of the ideas generated. Have people take turns reading one of the guidelines aloud until all have been read.

   Give each person a copy of Handout 11–5: Breakthrough Generator Matrix and explain how the matrix functions. Work through two examples about how to improve communication using words chosen somewhat at random from the matrix. For example:

   a. **speed/social connection/rearrange**—*Ideas:* Create pods or neighborhoods of people who need to access and share information rapidly. Surround them with white boards, cork boards, and other surfaces for posting information.

b. **fun/stories/individualize**—*Ideas:* Invite people to invent fantasy stories about what might be and then post those stories on the Internet.

Have participants at each table pick one word from each column and brainstorm ideas related to the challenge statement. Ask them to write one idea per sticky note. Give them five to 10 minutes to generate ideas. Call time and ask someone at each table to tell the large group what words they chose and what ideas were stimulated. They should attach their ideas to a sheet of flipchart paper as they read them aloud.

Learning Activity 10–5: BrainwritingPlus

This activity introduces one of the simplest tools to use in generating a lot of ideas quickly, especially with a group that may not be completely familiar with brainstorming and idea-generation techniques. BrainwritingPlus gives you a quick way to generate a quantity of focused ideas.

TARGET AUDIENCE

The target audience for this activity is any group that wants to brainstorm ideas about an issue. (Energy is always higher if the brainstorming can be done around a real topic, even such a general one as how to improve communication or how to contribute to the community.) This activity is also ideal for teams working on a specific innovation project because they already have a topic and the motivation to make progress on it.

GOALS AND OBJECTIVES

The goals and objectives of this activity are to

- build a better understanding of the Creativity element of the InnovationDNA

- increase participants' understanding of brainstorming and the skills it requires

- provide a tool for generating a lot of ideas

- provide experience using the tool.

MATERIALS

For the instructor:

- Several poster-sized copies of Handout 11–6: Better Brainstorming Guidelines, placed around the room

- Handout 11–7: BrainwritingPlus—Powerful and Easy!

For the participants:

- Handout 11–6: Better Brainstorming Guidelines, one copy for each attendee

◆ Handout 11–7: BrainwritingPlus—Powerful and Easy! (either the worksheet with Random Words or the one with Scamper Plus words), one worksheet for each person

TIME

◆ 15–25 minutes

INSTRUCTIONS

1. Prior to the session, pick an issue of interest to people. Examples that generally interest most people are how to reduce costs in a certain area, how to enhance customer satisfaction, or how to improve communication. (For more ideas about how to develop a challenge statement that will interest people, see Learning Activity 10–4: Breakthrough Generator.)

2. Explain the following points about *brainstorming:*

   ◆ Although it is the most widely used *term* for idea generation, few people know how to use it well.

   ◆ It is a simple process, but there are some basic guidelines that are very important. Research has proven than merely reading the guidelines aloud before generating ideas increases both the quantity and quality of ideas.

   ◆ One problem with brainstorming is that it requires diversity—different levels of expertise and experience, different perspectives and backgrounds, different thinking styles, and so on. That very diversity, however, can intimidate people and limit their participation. If a novice is in the room with an expert, he or she may not want to look foolish or inexperienced and so will not voice thoughts freely. An introvert who may need more time to form thoughts can easily be overshadowed by an extrovert who "thinks with his or her mouth open."

3. Describe *brainwriting* as a specific form of brainstorming that enables people to think on their own and to suggest ideas anonymously. It allows them to proceed at their own speed and offers them an opportunity to build on other people's ideas.

4. Explain that you want the participants to experience the process of brainwriting so you have developed a simple challenge to work with for the next few minutes. Ask if they are willing to do that and then present the challenge.

5. Ask various participants to read each point of the Better Brainstorming Guidelines.

6. Make sure everyone has a BrainwritingPlus worksheet and read the instructions to them.

7. Give participants several minutes to generate ideas around the chosen topic.

8. Call time and have people count and report the number of ideas on their sheets. Add up the total number and congratulate them for generating so many ideas in such a short amount of time.

DEBRIEFING

Questions for debriefing might include the following:

1. What reactions did you have to the process of brainwriting?

2. How and when might you use this tool?

Learning Activity 10–6: Think 360

This learning activity presents a structured way to look at all the factors around an issue, new concept, or possible solution to avoid being blindsided by them later.

TARGET AUDIENCE

This is a useful activity for anyone who wants to know how to make ideas more powerful and to make sure those ideas can be implemented effectively.

GOALS AND OBJECTIVES

The goals and objectives of this activity are to

- build a better understanding of the Communication element of the InnovationDNA

- offer a systematic way of thinking and communicating about all aspects of a situation

- provide a worksheet that will stimulate conversation.

MATERIALS

For the participants:

- Handout 11–8: Think 360 worksheet

TIME

- 10–30 minutes

INSTRUCTIONS

1. Prior to the session, pick an issue to focus on—perhaps something general like how to reduce costs in a certain area or how to improve customer satisfaction, or some more specific topic. Because this session will not try to solve the problem or reach a conclusion, the topic should be one that people will be willing to think about for a period of time. If this activity follows a brainstorming session, groups may choose to explore further one of the ideas they generated there.

2. Explain that a common problem in innovation is jumping into implementation too quickly. Think 360 is a systematic way to think and communicate about all aspects of an issue.

3. Introduce the topic to be considered. Explain that although there are a multitude of aspects to any problem or opportunity they tend to fall into some standard categories:

   ◆ people

   ◆ resources

   ◆ timing

   ◆ customers

   ◆ trends

   ◆ competitors

   ◆ use

   ◆ convenience

   ◆ environment.

4. Break the large group up into smaller groups of three or four participants.

5. Pass out copies of Handout 11–8: Think 360 worksheet, one to each participant.

6. Explain that during this session the groups aren't going to try to solve the problem or reach a conclusion; rather they are going to talk about each category and the specific questions on the worksheet. Instruct them to note which categories are most important to the focus issue and decide when they would want to ask the questions and develop answers.

7. Allow discussion to continue until there are about four minutes left in the time allotted and then debrief the activity.

Learning Activity 10-7: Quadrant Collaboration

Use this simple but powerful technique to bring order out of the chaos created when groups brainstorm a sticky-note blizzard of ideas.

TARGET AUDIENCE

This activity suits general audiences who need to make decisions more effectively and innovation project teams who have generated a quantity of new possibilities and who need to begin the process of evaluating them.

GOALS AND OBJECTIVES

The goals and objectives of this learning activity are to

- build a better understanding of the Collaboration element of the InnovationDNA

- provide participants with a simple tool for doing a rough-order sort on a multitude of ideas

- give people experience using the tool.

MATERIALS

For the participants:

- Handout 11-9: Quadrant Collaboration

- quantity of ideas on sticky notes or BrainwritingPlus sheets created in a previous session.

- one sheet of flipchart paper to be used by each group of three to four people or each innovation project team

- markers

For groups that have not already generated a quantity of ideas:

- Handout 11-10: Improving Innovation Ideas, one set for each table or team

- Scissors for each table

TIME

- 15–30 minutes

INSTRUCTIONS

1. Read Handout 11–9 so that you are familiar with the process and can guide the group through the activity.

2. Break the large group into small groups of three or four people. Give each group a copy of Handout 11–10: Improving Innovation Ideas.

3. Explain to participants that the groups have been selected to serve on a committee helping the organization create its future through innovation. The company is counting on them to stimulate innovation and develop a culture that supports it. So far, however, the committee has not been given a budget and members still have their normal jobs to do. Last week the committee held a brainstorming session and came up with lots of ideas that could be implemented on a small budget and without extensive time commitments.

4. Tell participants that their task this week is to sort the ideas they generated and find some that could make a difference in the company's future. Each group should be working with individual ideas.

5. The first task is to do a rough sort to cull the ideas they don't like at all. Encourage them to pick no more than 10 ideas to take to the next step. This should take only three to four minutes. *Groups that have not generated ideas previously will use Handout 11–10: Improving Innovation Ideas. These sheets should be cut apart so that the group has 36 separate ideas. Cut the ideas on Handout 11–10 apart so that the group has 36 separate ideas to work with.*

6. On the flipchart paper draw a basic quadrant diagram and explain that this process is a way to roughly agree on where a concept falls when measured against two different criteria. This is not a time for precise analysis. Explain that right now the groups are operating on "faux facts," things that they believes are true but that would have to be verified prior to making major decisions.

7. Explain that the first step when using the Quadrant tool is to choose the criteria for each axis. (For this activity use "Feasibility" and "Payoff." The quadrant diagram you draw should resemble Tool 10–1, with different criteria.)

Tool 10–1
Quadrant Chart Example

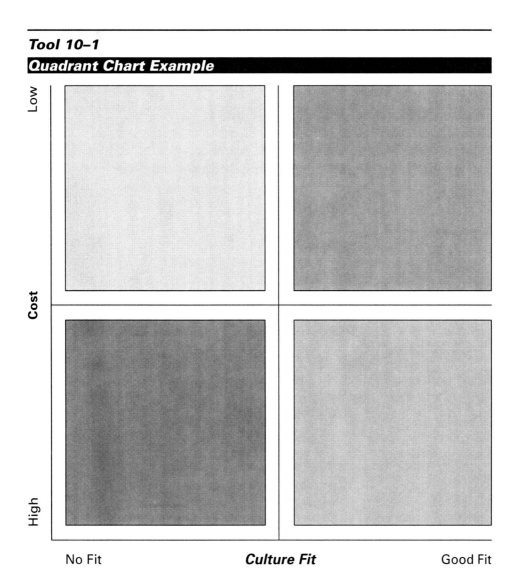

8. Have each group draw on its sheet of flipchart paper a quadrant diagram with "Feasibility" on the vertical axis and "Payoff" on the horizontal axis.

9. Using Handout 11–9 as a guide, groups should begin to put their ideas on the quadrant they just drew. If there are just a few ideas and they are on sticky notes, putting them on the chart is simple. But if there are a lot of ideas written up in various ways, it may make more sense to number each idea card, note, sheet, or write-up and then enter that number with a couple of key words on the quadrant diagram.

10. Continue to emphasize that this is a rough sort rather than an in-depth analysis. Give groups several minutes to chart their ideas, reserving some time for debriefing the process.

Learning Activity 10–8: Innovation Criteria Grid

This activity is a powerful thinking process for people who want to validate a new concept.

TARGET AUDIENCE

The target audience includes anyone who wants to understand the process of validating ideas and make them more powerful and successful.

GOALS AND OBJECTIVES

The goals and objectives of this learning activity are to

- ◆ build a better understanding of the Completion element of the InnovationDNA

- ◆ emphasize the importance of setting criteria for evaluating ideas

- ◆ provide experience using the Criteria Grid to validate a concept.

MATERIALS

For the participants:

- ◆ Handout 11–10: Improving Innovation Ideas

- ◆ Handout 11–11: Innovation Criteria Grid worksheets

TIME

- ◆ 15–25 minutes

INSTRUCTIONS

1. Read Handout 11–11: Innovation Criteria Grid so that you are familiar enough with the process to guide participants through it. The three worksheets are examples of what might be developed in their actual work and are not intended to be formulas that they follow.

2. Break the large group into small groups of three or four people.

3. Explain that they have been selected to participate on a committee that is helping the organization create its future through innovation. The company is counting on the committee to stimulate innovation and develop a culture that supports it. To this point, however, they have not been given a budget and they still have their normal jobs to

do. At a brainstorming session last week they came up with a bunch of ideas that they thought were economical and not time intensive.

4. Tell groups that this week they are going to select the criteria for judging the ideas. Explain that setting criteria is one of the most difficult tasks facing innovation teams and that the Innovation Criteria Grid was developed to make the task easier.

5. Explain the three positions on the spectrum of innovation:

   a. **Improve** innovation seeks to cut costs, extend existing products, or make current processes more efficient.

   b. **Evolve** innovation leads to distinctly new and better products, services, or processes and should create new value for customers and/or the organization.

   c. **Transform** innovation focuses on creating new products, services, or processes that dramatically change everything, including the target market and value proposition.

6. Explain to participants that they should always determine what level of innovation they are trying to achieve. For this workshop activity, however, they are going to focus on "improve" and they are assuming that they currently have no budget or resources.

7. Ask participants to review the criteria on Handout 11–11: Innovation Criteria Grid worksheets and then discuss and answer the following questions:

   ◆ Which of the Improve criteria on the worksheet are appropriate for their current project?

   ◆ What additional criteria might be important?

   ◆ How would they rewrite or reword the ratings words?

8. Have them select an idea from Handout 11–10: Improving Innovation Ideas and work through the *Improve* worksheet in Handout 11–11.

9. Give participants several minutes to work in their small groups and then ask each group to present its results.

10. Discuss what additional criteria they used and which criteria didn't fit this project.

Learning Activity 10–9: Contemplation Matrix

This activity guides people through a process for thinking of simple and effective ways to share the lessons they have learned.

TARGET AUDIENCE

This activity is for anyone interested in creating ways to help people share lessons learned.

GOALS AND OBJECTIVES

The goals and objectives of this activity are to

- build a better understanding of the Contemplation element of the InnovationDNA

- emphasize the need to share information, ideas, and lessons

- help people find ways to share lessons they have learned.

MATERIALS

For the instructor:

- Easel, flipchart paper, markers

For the participants:

- Handout 11–12: Contemplation Matrix

TIME

- 15–25 minutes

INSTRUCTIONS

1. Read the Contemplation Matrix handout so that you are familiar enough with it to guide the participants through the activity.

2. Ask participants why it's important to share lessons learned and information gathered. Prompt them to talk about some ways they currently do this.

3. Ask them what the barriers are to sharing information in the organization, and list them on a sheet of flipchart paper mounted on the easel.

4. Have participants pair up and use Handout 11–12: Contemplation Matrix worksheet to think of possible ways to share new information, ideas, and insights. Give the pairs several minutes for this work.

5. Ask each pair to share the top three ideas it came up with. Capture those ideas on the flipchart paper as they are reported. Allow several minutes for discussion of the ideas they generated.

6. Ask people what they could do in their own departments to stimulate more sharing. Prompt a discussion and capture ideas.

Learning Activity 10–10: Are You Creative?

This quick activity teaches people to think about creativity in two ways so they can distinguish the innate creative potential from the social judgment of creativity.

TARGET AUDIENCE

This activity is appropriate for everyone who needs to understand the existence and importance of his or her own personal creativity.

GOALS AND OBJECTIVES

The goals and objectives of this learning activity are to

- ♦ help participants understand creativity as an innate part of human nature

- ♦ distinguish between creative potential and judged creativity.

MATERIALS

None required

TIME

- ♦ 5–10 minutes

INSTRUCTIONS

1. Ask participants to hold up their hands if they think they are creative. Then ask for a show of hands from those who think they are *not* creative.

2. Ask everyone to pretend to be someone else as they listen to the following story:

   Imagine that you live on an isolated island where there are no modern conveniences such as television, phones, faxes, computers, books, and so on. What you do have is an extremely fine set of art supplies left there earlier by a passing trade ship.

   You've always liked to paint scenes from your island—the birds, trees, people, clouds. You decide you need a new challenge so you go into a deep med-

*itation and you see a vision. Its beauty and power excite you and you begin
to paint and continue for days and weeks in a joyful frenzy.*

*When it's finished you show the painting to your friends and family. They
are stunned and call you a creative genius. They hang the painting in the
most prominent place on the island and people start commissioning you to
paint pictures for them. You become rich and famous on your island.*

*When a ship arrives one day and some passengers, come ashore the is-
landers lead them to where your painting hangs. You step closer, eagerly an-
ticipating their acclaim, but instead you hear, "Hey, look! Someone has
copied the 'Mona Lisa.'"*

3. Ask the participants what they believe happened to their status as
    creative geniuses at that point. (*Answer:* It probably plummeted with
    the islanders when they heard that the artist had copied someone
    else's painting and it had never existed at all with the visitors.)

4. Ask if the outcome had anything to do with them as talented artists
    or original thinkers. (*Answer:* No, it only involved the viewers' per-
    ceptions of the work.)

5. Tell participants that when they say they're not creative people, they
    might very well be right because no one can *be* a creative person; he
    or she can only be *perceived* as a creative person.

6. Explain that according to Mihaly Csikszentmihalyi in his book, *Cre-
    ativity,* there are three requirements for what we call "big-C" Creativity:

    a. **Field:** A field of endeavor such as art, music, science, business,
        architecture, and so on, which has a set of rules or norms.

    b. **Work:** Something (a book, painting, product, and the like) that
        goes beyond the rules or norms of the field.

    c. **Judges:** A group of people who know the rules and norms of the
        field, who see the work created, and who judge it to be novel and
        worthy.

7. Next explain that all of the participants who said they are creative
    are also right because "little-c" creativity is an inherent part of every
    human being. It's what we do. We create. We are creative beings. We
    create because it helps us survive and it feels good. It brings us joy.
    When we don't create, when we don't learn and grow, it brings us

pain. It deadens us. When this innate urge to create is thwarted or stifled we turn to unhealthy substitutes such as drugs, alcohol, crime, violence, and so on to lessen the pain.

8. Finally explain that the answer to the question "Are you creative?" is an overwhelming "yes!" All of us have the need and the capability to create and it has nothing to do with whether someone else labels us "creative."

Learning Activity 10–11: Three-Color Sorting

This is a simple tool that can be used to make a first cut in separating a large quantity of ideas.

TARGET AUDIENCE

This activity is useful for any group that has generated a large quantity of ideas that must be evaluated.

GOAL

The participants' goal for this activity is to learn a very simple technique for organizing quantities of ideas.

MATERIALS

- ◆ Red, yellow, and green dots (for small groups)

- ◆ Red, yellow, and green construction paper (for larger groups with more ideas to process)

TIME

- ◆ 10 minutes

INSTRUCTIONS

1. Ask the participants to identify a major evaluation category that can be linked to the commonly understood meanings of red–yellow–green, that is, stop–caution–go. The category they select might be Payoff, Newness, Uniqueness, Doability, Alignment with Strategy, Trends, Criteria, or something similar.

2. Have them establish the specific designations. Here are some examples:

   - ◆ **Payoff**—red = low, yellow = uncertain, green = high

   - ◆ **Newness**—red = heard of before, tried before, not new; yellow = some new elements; green = definitely new

3. *If you are working with a small group of people who already generated some ideas in a previous activity, make sure the ideas are on individual sheets of paper or sticky notes. Ask participants to sort the ideas into*

color categories as rapidly as possible. Have everyone put the appropriate colored dot on each idea.

4. *With a large group and larger quantities of ideas,* divide the group into smaller groups of 10 or fewer participants and divide the ideas (which should be on individual sheets or sticky notes) among the groups. (Another way to speed the process is to put three sheets of construction paper on each table—red, yellow, and green. Ask each person to take several ideas and sort them onto the colored sheets according to the evaluation criteria chosen.)

Slide 10–1

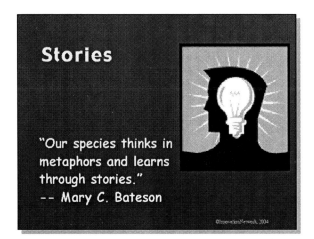

Slide 10–2

Slide 10–3

Slide 10–4

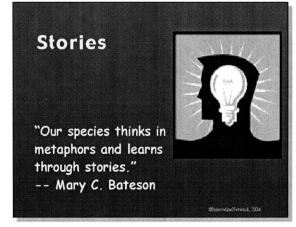

Handouts

What's in This Chapter?

- Worksheets designed for use with innovation workshop learning activities

- Resource handouts that serve as reminders of topics covered in the workshops

This chapter includes all of the handouts that are used for the trainings. The same handouts are on the accompanying CD and maybe printed easily from that format. You will find each of them identified by number as identified as Handout 11–*[number]*.pdf.

Handout 11–1

What's Your Thinking Style?

Some people love to start new projects but run out of steam before they're finished. Others love to bring order out of chaos and they enjoy the feeling of completion that comes with a job well done. Some people love to present new ideas and help people see connections in new ways. Others love to tinker with concepts and gadgets, taking them apart and putting them back together again.

Each of us has our own unique thinking style. Understanding how we think can help us build on our strengths and know when we need to build partnerships with others to fill in our gaps. Having a preferred thinking style does not mean that we can't use the other thinking styles. We often become very proficient at developing skills in areas that do not represent our naturally preferred style. However, using our preferred thinking style generally energizes us, whereas using the other styles may drain our energy or be more difficult to sustain over time.

Understanding the thinking styles of others can help us work more productively on teams. When we understand the importance and contribution of each thinking style, we can deliberately create diversity on our project teams. Research has shown that project teams comprising diverse thinking styles create better results faster.

There are many great thinking style assessment tools. One that we like a lot is the Herrmann Brain Dominance Instrument (HBDI). Taking the full assessment is most helpful, but you can quickly gather clues about your thinking styles by asking yourself or others two simple questions that reflect different mindsets that influence your outlook on innovation. (Again, this is about what energizes you, not what skills or proficiencies you have developed.)

The first question addresses your timeframe mindset: start (present) or finish (future)? The figure to the left represents the two options.

Question: *Are you more energized when you are starting a new project or when you are organizing and completing an ongoing project?*

The second question involves your challenge mindset: fix it or sell it? The top figure on the next page represents those two choices.

Question: *Are you more energized when you are sharing, presenting, or selling concepts or when you are researching, analyzing, or refining concepts?*

These two questions can be mapped into a quadrant (see the bottom figure on the next page) to help you understand your own thinking style and the thinking styles of others.

continued on next page

Handout 11–1, continued
What's Your Thinking Style?

Identifying where you fall on the spectrum for each question will determine which quadrant(s) represents your preferred thinking style. So, if you said you prefer to finish projects and fix problems, your preferred thinking style would wind up in the green "organizing" box.

The following descriptions are brief overviews to help you understand the different thinking styles. Remember: these are descriptions of what *energizes* you, not descriptions of your skills. Thinking styles are defined in terms of color as a match to the colorized version of the thinking styles graphic that appears on the CD.

* **Blue Thinkers (Problem Solving)** are always looking for problems to solve. They like to deal with facts and quantitative data. They tend to be more objective and logical than are Yellow Thinkers and more future oriented than Green Thinkers. *Strength:* problem solving. *Weakness:* process and empathetic communication.

* **Green Thinkers (Organizing)** love bringing order out of chaos and making processes better. They like to deal with objects and reality and tend to be more practical and concrete than Red Thinkers and better at finishing tasks than Yellow Thinkers. *Strength:* order and process. *Weakness:* knowing when to let go and how to communicate benefits.

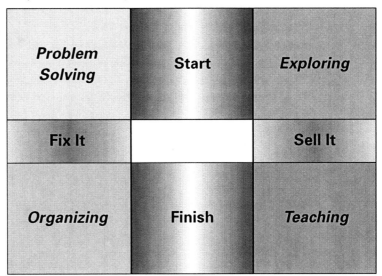

Adapted from the Whole Brain Model, copyright held by the Ned Hermann Group, Inc.

* **Red Thinkers (Teaching)** thrive on sharing and presenting information in a way that leads to a natural close of a deal or a project. They are more focused on sharing current projects and information with the world than are Green Thinkers and less interested in developing new concepts than Yellow Thinkers. *Strength:* collaborative selling. *Weakness:* bulletproofing concepts and logical problem solving.

* **Yellow Thinkers (Exploring)** love finding new possibilities and exploring the world. They tend to see the big picture and synthesize information but find it more difficult to

continued on next page

Handout 11–1, continued
What's Your Thinking Style?

handle final details than do the Red Thinkers and are more apt to overlook important facts or flaws than are the Blue Thinkers. *Strength:* embracing change. *Weakness:* too much shooting from the hip and not enough follow-up.

Additional Resources

◆ *Herrmann Brain Dominance Instrument:* Originally developed by Ned Herrmann, the HBDI is one of the oldest and most validated assessment tools available. For more information, go to http://www.hbdi.com.

◆ *Diversity Game:* Ted Coulson and Alison Strickland, with Applied Creativity, have developed a fun group activity based on the HBDI. Information is available at http://www.appliedcreativityinc.com/book_diversity.html.

◆ *Team Dimensions Profile* (formerly Innovate with C.A.R.E): This profile identifies the natural team roles of different thinking styles: creator, advancer, refiner, and executor. Visit this site for more information: http://www.corexcel.com/html/care.desc.htm.

◆ **Kirton Adaptor–Innovator (KAI):** This assessment of creativity style developed by Michael Kirton is based on a model that identifies people as having a natural tendency toward either adaptation or innovation. If you like to use the Myers-Briggs Type Indicator (MBTI), take a look at the following site for a good article that matches the MBTI with the KAI: http://www.tri-network.com/articles/kaimbti.html.

◆ **Innovation Styles:** This profile explores innovation styles in terms of Visioning, Exploring, Experimenting, and Modifying. It is an online assessment and that makes it easy to administer. A unique aspect of this system is that it relates creativity tools to the different styles. For more information: http://www.creativeadvantage.com.

Handout 11–2
Metaphorical Thinking

For many of us the joy of metaphor was squashed by a fourth-grade English teacher who kept harping (and grading us!) on the difference between metaphor and simile. Well, we're adults now and we can stop thinking about the trivial stuff so we are using "metaphor" as the general term. We think by making connections, linking one thing to another in a way that reveals to us the essence of each.

Research shows that we think in metaphors and that finding a metaphor for something is how we begin to truly perceive it. Try to describe something new to someone who can't see what you're describing. Listen for how quickly you start to say "It's like a. . . . " Until you find the metaphor, the person you're describing something to can't see it.

The following bulleted items are exercises in metaphorical thinking. Before beginning any of them, relax and prepare to have fun!

- Think about your life—What's it like? Perhaps it's most like an ocean, a kaleidoscope, a fine wine, or a jigsaw puzzle with too many pieces and no picture to guide you?

- Pick any two objects in the room and start to think about one by thinking of the qualities of the other. Suppose you looked at a book and your telephone, and you wanted to know more about your telephone by thinking about the qualities of the book. The book is made of paper covered with ink. The book is easily disposed of after use but sometimes it takes on great value because of its content or rareness. If you were trying to improve the phone, these qualities of the book might suggest improvements such as disposable phones, replaceable phone "coverplates," or phones that become collector's items. This short exercise may not have produced highly original ideas but they are different from what you might have thought of by just focusing on the phone.

- Think of a problem you have or a situation you would like to change, and pick an image as a metaphor for how you feel about the problem or situation. Think through the qualities of the metaphor you picked and see how it relates to your situation. See if thinking of it this way brings you any insights.

Slide 11–1

- When you come to a new situation, ask "What is this like?" See if you can find a connection that will help you think more deeply about the situation.

- When you start a new project, think of a metaphor for the outcome you would like to achieve. This is especially powerful if your group can come up with a metaphor. Find an image that captures the sense of the metaphor and put it up where everyone can see it.

Handout 11–3
Springboard Stories

Through a story, life invites us to come inside as a participant. — Stephen Denning

In 1997 Stephen Denning was frustrated in his efforts to create a knowledge management system to help the World Bank share information globally. He had made numerous presentations with impeccably logical charts and graphs. His audiences routinely nodded their heads "yes" but did nothing. Then he heard the following 29-word story from a co-worker:

> *In June, 1995 a health worker in Kamana, Zambia, logged onto the Centers for Disease Control Website and got the answer to a question on how to treat malaria.*

Denning began to tell this story as part of his presentations, and the response of his listeners changed. They began to see the future and the possibilities for what he was proposing. In his book *The Springboard,* he describes these stories as "less a vehicle for communication of large amounts of information and more a tiny fuse that ignites a new story in the listeners' minds, which establishes new connections and patterns in the listeners' existing information, attitudes and perceptions."

Springboard stories are carefully crafted to ignite new action. They free the imagination and invite the listener to see herself or himself in a better future. They build a sense of confidence and a mindset of action.

Here are the seven basic principles for these gem-like stories:

1. The story must have a beginning, middle, and end that is relevant to the listeners.

2. It must be highly compressed—remember, the original springboard story was only 29 words long.

3. It must have a hero, a person who accomplished something noteworthy.

4. There must be a surprising element. The story should shock the listener out of his or her complacency, shake up the listener's model of reality.

5. It must stimulate an "of course!" reaction; that is, when the surprise is delivered, the listener should see the obvious path to the future.

6. It must illustrate the change process desired, be relatively recent, and "pretty much" true.

7. It must have a happy ending.

For more information about springboard stories, visit Denning's Website, www.stevedenning.com.

Handout 11–4
Cracking Questions

A great question can unravel a mystery like a kitten batting a ball of twine. Finding those great questions that open minds and the secrets of the universe is a learned skill based on understanding the purposes of the questions and on practice.

Here are four purposes and 20 questions. You'll probably find other great questions as you begin to practice your questioning skills.

- **Purpose #1. Open the Future.** Ask questions that open up thought, imagination, and conversation about future possibilities.
- **Purpose #2. Reveal New Territory.** Ask questions that take us somewhere...to new information, people, resources, ideas, or perspectives.
- **Purpose #3. Fill In the Blanks.** Ask questions that expose thinking gaps.
- **Purpose #4. Find the Heart.** Ask questions that explore emotional connections.

Questions for Purpose #1, Future

1. What is the hole in the universe that is waiting to be filled?

2. What would make customers (internal or external) say "Wow!"?

3. If we had a magic wand and could choose to make anything happen, what would it be?

4. Wouldn't it be great if we. . . ? Or, Wouldn't it be awful if. . . ?

5. What is the world our hearts long for?

6. Two years from now, if we were celebrating our success, what would have happened?

Questions for Purpose #2, New Territory

7. How might we find new information about the issue?

8. If we could change one thing about this, what would it be?

9. What person, living or dead, would have a completely different perspective or new information on this project?

10. What is the absolute core, the most basic element of this issue? Or, what absolutely can't be changed?

11. What resources might we be overlooking?

12. With whom could we form partnerships to become more effective?

13. How might we make it [*better, bigger, faster, smaller, more fun*]?

continued on next page

Handout 11–4, continued

Cracking Questions

Questions for Purpose #3, Filling In the Blanks

14. What assumptions are we making? Or, what are we not giving ourselves permission to do? Or, what rules have we never questioned?

15. How is the world changing?

16. What are our blindspots?

17. What is unfinished about this?

Questions for Purpose #4, Heart

18. What will we do with our one wild and precious life?

19. What do we personally want from participation in this project? Or, what is our passionate purpose?

20. What is it about this project that wakes us up in the morning filled with excitement?

Handout 11–5
Breakthrough Generator Matrix

Innovation may seem like a mysterious process but there are techniques that help simplify it. The matrix below encourages you to think about your product or service from your customers' perspective, specifically considering the benefits most important to them.

To use the matrix, pick one of the primary benefits in column 1 and a secondary benefit from column 2. Then put them together into a "How might we...?" statement. For instance, "How might we improve our packaging by making it more friendly?" Or, "How might we justify a higher price by adding more information or an educational component?" You can also combine two primary benefits or two secondary benefits. "How might we improve our packaging by making it more dependable?" Or, "How might we improve the image of our service by including stories?"

Then pick an action and apply it to the statement. For instance, take Substitute as the action: "What could we substitute on our packaging to make it more friendly?" Or take Partner as the action: "Who could we partner with to justify a higher price by adding more information and an educational component?"

Use the matrix to develop several intriguing questions before beginning the process of idea generation. Pick the one question that has the most energy around it and begin to develop ideas about how to achieve it.

Breakthrough Generator Matrix

PRIMARY BENEFITS	SECONDARY BENEFITS	ACTION
Size	Image/Status	Add
Speed	Information/Education	Subtract
Convenience	Social connection	Rearrange
Durability	Texture	Outsource
Fuel Efficiency	Shape	Minimize/Maximize
Safety	Emotion	Standardize
Quality	Nostalgia	Individualize
Price	Smell	Extend
Dependability	Color	Combine
Ease of use	Excitement	Substitute

continued on next page

Handout 11–5, continued

Breakthrough Generator Matrix

Matrix (continued)

PRIMARY BENEFITS	SECONDARY BENEFITS	ACTION
Distribution	Beauty	Adapt
Fun	Stories	Modify
Experience	Interactivity	Reverse
Packaging	Flexibility	Use in a new way
Variety of choice	Friendliness	Partner

Handout 11-6
Better Brainstorming Guidelines

If you want more and better ideas, post and review these guidelines for brainstorming at the beginning of a session. Studies show that this simple step can improve results by 50 percent, giving you more and better ideas. The most important guideline happens before you walk into the room—Deliberate Diversity; that is, make sure you have a diverse mix of thinking styles, backgrounds, perspectives, and skills represented in your brainstorming group.

- **Judge Later.** During the idea-generation process there should be no judgment or discussion—not even groans, frowns, or "great idea!" remarks. Just keep pumping out the ideas and go for quantity, not quality. The judging process will come later.

- **Avoid Discussion.** Avoid stories, discussions, and elaborations on how the idea could be done or how great it might be. Just keep generating ideas.

- **Capture Ideas.** Have someone record every idea expressed, have each person write her or his ideas on sticky notes (one idea per sheet), or employ some other capture process.

- **Be Specific.** Every idea should be specific and actionable—no generalities such as "improve communication." Each idea should include a noun and a verb, such as "distribute a weekly newsletter."

- **Build.** Build on other people's ideas; make them bigger, smaller, or a different color, or turn them inside out. Say, "Yes, and...." For instance, "Yes, and we could distribute it by email or in payroll envelopes."

- **Participate.** Ideas come from anywhere and everywhere. The best idea may be in the mind of someone who has never, ever volunteered an idea before so it's important for everyone to contribute all of their ideas.

- **Set Time Limit.** Set a time limit for generating ideas, preferably not more than 30–45 minutes. At the end of this time, take a short break and assess where you are.

- **Number Your Ideas.** IDEO, the award-winning international corporate design firm, believes that numbering ideas stimulates the flow of ideas. In its opinion, 100 ideas per hour indicates a good, fluid brainstorming session.

Handout 11-7
BrainwritingPlus: Powerful and Easy!

Brainwriting is one of the simplest idea-generation techniques and often creates some breakthrough ideas as people build on the ideas of others. It works best with small groups of five to nine people and two of the three worksheets provided here include stimulator words to make it an even more powerful tool. Here are the guidelines:

Reminders:

1. Review the issue or purpose for the session.

2. Develop in advance the criteria for success.

3. Work silently (discussion will follow the ideation time).

4. Be specific. Every idea should have a subject and a verb; for example, "create a weekly newsletter."

5. Don't judge ideas. Quantity counts.

6. Build on ideas, reverse them, and turn them inside out or upside down.

Generating Ideas:

1. Print out a worksheet for each person and distribute them to everyone participating in the session.

2. Each person writes one idea in each of the three boxes of one line.

3. When a person has filled in one line of three boxes, he or she puts the sheet in the center of the group's table and takes a new worksheet from those in the center of the table.

4. Each person adds three more ideas to each sheet taken, building on ideas where appropriate or just adding new ideas as they occur.

5. Allow 20–30 minutes or stop when it's obvious that energy is lagging.

Processing Ideas: *(With more than nine people, break into subgroups.)*

1. Establish or review criteria for success.

2. Each person takes one sheet and marks an "X" beside the ideas that are interesting.

3. Participants exchange sheets and mark interesting ideas, repeating the exchange until everyone has seen three sheets. Ask participants to hold on to the third sheet they process.

continued on next page

Handout 11-7, continued
BrainwritingPlus: Powerful and Easy!

4. From the worksheet she or he is holding, each person reads the ideas that have three Xs, then the ones with 2 Xs, and then those with a single X.

5. Look for any "orphan" ideas—those for which someone has a lot of passion around but that no one considered interesting.

6. Cut the ideas apart and tape or glue the ideas that received votes onto index cards.

7. Tape the index cards onto flipchart sheets in order of priorities—3 Xs together on one sheet, 2 Xs on another sheet, and so on. Have everyone walk around and reread the ideas. Begin a discussion about which ideas are best and ways to make them even stronger.

Judging Ideas:

1. Review the criteria again.

2. Use the process presented in Handout 11–9: Quadrant Collaboration to create a quadrant to help you map the ideas generated against two important criteria.

3. Use Handout 11–14: Dot Voting with a Difference to select one or two ideas to develop further.

BRAINWRITING WORKSHEETS

On the following pages you will find three Brainwriting Worksheets, with directions for use. Choose whichever worksheet best fits your situation. The first one is the Basic Brainwriting Worksheet. It has empty cells for participants to fill. The second sheet is the Brainwriting Worksheet with Random Words. The third one if the Brainwriting Worksheet with SCAMPER Plus.

continued on next page

Basic Brainwriting Worksheet

Instructions: Take one worksheet and enter three ideas, one in each box on a horizontal line. Then put this sheet in the center of the table. Take a different worksheet from the table and enter three new ideas horizontally. If you start to run out of ideas, build on the ideas already on the sheet.

continued on next page

Brainwriting Worksheet with Random Words

*Instructions:*Take one worksheet and enters three ideas, one in each box on a horizontal line. Then, put that sheet in the center of the table, take a different sheet from the table, and enter three new ideas. Use the words in the box to stimulate ideas—or ignore them if you're on a roll. If you start to run out of ideas, build on the ideas already on the sheet.

Speed	Convenience	Color
Communication	Love	Partnership
Size	Fun	Star
Door	Beauty	Excitement
Water	Durability	Texture

continued on next page

Brainwriting Worksheet with SCAMPER* Plus

Instructions: take one worksheet and enter three ideas, one in each box on a horizontal line. Then put that sheet in the center of the table, take a different sheet, and enter three new ideas. Use the words in the box to stimulate ideas, or ignore them if you're on a roll. If you start to run out of ideas, build on the ideas already on the sheet.

Subtract	Combine	Adapt
Partner	Extend	Reverse
Rearrange	Standardize	Add
Minimize	Individualize	Substitute
Enlarge	Colorize	Beautify
Simplify	Magnify	Eliminate

SCAMPER is a term and process developed by Michael Michalko building on earlier work by Alex Osborn. Michalko's terms included Substitute, Combine, Adapt, Modify, Put (to another use), Eliminate, Reverse.

Handout 11–8

Think 360

When you are trying to make a decision or choose among many options, it helps to have a structured method of looking at the entire system surrounding the decision. The first step is to consider which factors affect and are affected by the decision. Every situation is different and will include unique factors.

The list below offers a few major factors with sample questions for each. Be certain to consider every problem or opportunity separately and make sure you are looking at each important factor.

You may not have time to consider each factor in depth or to complete the worksheet provided here, but at least scan the worksheet.

Major Factors and Pertinent Questions

- **People:** Who will it affect? Who needs to be involved or informed? Who has information that might be critical? Who could sabotage the project? Whose availability is critical?

- **Resources:** What resources are critical to success? What might make critical resources unavailable? What new resources will be needed?

- **Timing:** What deadlines are critical to success? What calendar events might affect the schedule? Whose availability is critical? What potential delays might throw off the entire project?

- **Customers:** What is critically important to customers? What are they emotionally attached to? What features are they willing to live without?

- **Trends:** What new technologies, demographics, government regulations, or economic changes might affect this project?

- **Competitors:** What are the competitors doing? What new competitors are developing?

- **Use:** How will it be used? Are there any hazardous materials involved? Could someone be injured in the use? Is it comfortable?

- **Convenience:** What would make it more user friendly? Will customers be able to obtain it easily? How will it be serviced and supported?

- **Environment:** How will it affect the environment? How will it affect the local community?

continued on next page

Think 360 Worksheet

Instructions: Use this worksheet to describe the system that surrounds the decision you are making. Consider the factors and questions carefully and address those that are appropriate for your situation. Space is provided for as many as three answers to each question. Add your own questions as needed.

FACTORS AND QUESTIONS	ANSWER #1	ANSWER #2	ANSWER #3
People			
Who will it affect? (individuals, groups, departments, and so forth)			
Who needs to be involved or informed?			
Who has information that might be critical?			
Who could sabotage the project?			
Whose availability is critical?			
Who will make the decision?			
Resources			
What resources are critical to success?			
What might make critical resources unavailable?			
What new resources might be needed?			
Where can it be made most effectively?			

continued on next page

Think 360 Worksheet, continued

FACTORS AND QUESTIONS	ANSWER #1	ANSWER #2	ANSWER #3
Timing			
What deadlines are critical to success?			
What calendar events might affect the schedule?			
What potential delays might throw off the entire project?			
What are the "go/no-go" points?			
Customers			
What is critically important to customers?			
What changes in customer needs and wants might affect the project?			
How will customers know about the change?			
Trends			
What new technology might affect the project?			
What demographics might affect the project?			
What government regulations might affect the project?			

continued on next page

Think 360 Worksheet, continued

FACTORS AND QUESTIONS	ANSWER #1	ANSWER #2	ANSWER #3
What changes in the economy might affect the project?			
Competitors			
What are the competitors doing?			
What new competitors are developing?			
Use			
How will it be used?			
Are there any hazardous materials involved?			
Is it comfortable?			
Convenience			
What would make it more user friendly?			
Will customers be able to obtain it easily?			
How will it be serviced and supported?			

continued on next page

Think 360 Worksheet, continued

FACTORS AND QUESTIONS	ANSWER #1	ANSWER #2	ANSWER #3
Environment			
How will it affect the environment?			
How will it affect the local community?			

Handout 11–9
Quadrant Collaboration

After you've generated a ton of ideas, what do you do with them? The one thing you *don't* want to do is send all of those sticky notes off with someone assigned to type up a report.

Quadrant Collaboration can bring order out of chaos and give you a running start on knowing which ideas should be implemented and in what order.

Here are the seven steps of Quadrant Collaboration:

1. **Pick Major Criteria.** Think about two criteria for judging your ideas. Two common ones are "Feasibility" and "Payoff."

Tool 11–1
Quadrant Chart Example

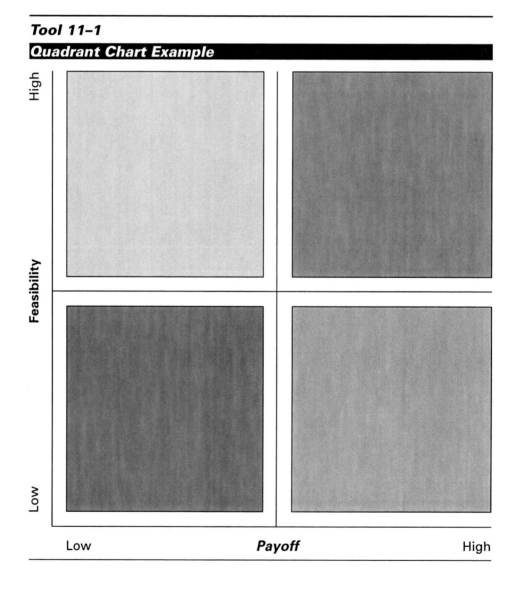

continued on next page

Handout 11–9, continued

Quadrant Collaboration

2. **Draw the Quadrants.** On a flipchart pad draw a square and divide it into quadrants by inserting two perpendicular axes. Label the vertical axis "Feasibility" with "Low" at the bottom and "High" at the top. Label the horizontal axis "Payoff" with "Low" at the left and "High" at the right. (See Tool 11–1.)

   You can experiment with other terms for the axes. "Feasibility" might be changed to "Implementation Time" or "Effort" or "Cost." "Payoff" might be changed to "Excitement" or "Value" or "Potential."

3. **Use Faux Facts.** Have everyone agree that you're just going to use the tool to do a rough-order evaluation of the idea. This is not the time for analysis and science or for lengthy debate. Thinking of this evaluation as "faux facts" with analysis to come later helps people make judgments more quickly.

4. **Position the Ideas.** As rapidly as possible, put the ideas on the quadrants in a way that reflects the general agreement of the group. If there are too many ideas to put on the chart, have each individual pick their five favorite ideas and put them up.

5. **Reflect.** Tell everyone to step back and think about where the ideas wound up on the chart and make any final adjustments.

6. **Determine Needs.** Talk about each quadrant in relationship to your specific situation. If you need a quick success, you want the easiest idea with the highest payoff. If you're looking for your next-generation success, you want the highest payoff that appears to be at least potentially doable.

7. **Select Ideas.** Identify the ideas with the highest level of excitement and take those ideas into the next level of project planning.

Handout 11–10
Improving Innovation Ideas

Have a "Failure Party" at which people share their worst idea or biggest failure. Encourage management participation. Make it fun.

Print out the Innovation-DNA Framework of Principles and post it prominently where it will remind others of innovation. Make sure it's in all meeting rooms.

Stimulate conversations around innovation in meetings, in the halls, wherever you can.

Create your own email list of people who understand how important innovation is. Email them short, interesting articles or stories to sustain their interest.

Model innovation. Make sure people see you taking on new challenges, making mistakes, honoring ideas, being collaborative, and taking time to learn the lessons from the projects you finish.

Make your office an innovation magnet. Make it colorful and fun with books, tapes, toys, and models or graphic representations of projects. (Chocolate helps, too!)

Start an innovation group and talk about how you can spread innovation to the tipping point!

Pick a book about creativity and start an innovation book club.

Ask some of your co-workers how they define innovation and then talk about what gets in your way of doing it.

Send an innovation article to your boss and ask if you can meet to talk about it.

Start an innovation book shelf in your office. Invite people to borrow the books. (Be prepared to lose them.)

Share articles and stories about what innovation looks like in your own organization and in other organizations.

At every meeting ask, "Are we being innovative?" Or, "Is there a better way to do this?"

Always ask, "What else could we do?" when thinking about projects or problems.

Always ask, "Does this support our vision? Does this create value for our customers?" when thinking about projects.

Share examples of innovative ideas related to your business and get innovators on the same page.

In a meeting, carve out a "total agreement" time, at which point all ideas must be agreed with and built on to find the "greatness" in them. No negativity allowed!

Make a provocative poster that reads, "Rumor has it that our competitors are making time for innovation."

Send an email with the start of a storyline about a success in the organization and have people add to it.

continued on next page

Handout 11–10, continued
Improving Innovation Ideas

Hold a "dump old ideas" brown-bag lunch. Ask, "What's one thing we can stop doing so we have more time for innovation?" Then determine how actions can be taken on the best ideas.

Ask employees to create a "Perfect World" wall graphic. Use it to stimulate conversation about how to make the work environment a more perfect world.

Produce an Innovation Fair at which people create posters or displays of innovation projects that have been completed or that they are working on and would like help with.

Declare a "Purple-Idea Day" during which people generate really far-out ideas. Or declare a "Red-Idea Day" for those ideas that are too hot to handle. Carry the color scheme throughout. When ideas are gathered, you might publish the "Purple Sheet" or the "Red News" to management.

Form Idea Teams— groups that meet for one coffee break each week to generate ideas on specified topics. (This might also be a way to get people to work with people outside their normal work group.)

Hold an Innovation Story Hour during which people tell stories of innovation processes they've been involved in. Identify the principles behind these stories and talk about how to create an environment that supports innovation.

Hold a "What Could We Do to *Prevent* Creativity and Innovation?" brainstorming session. Then do the opposite.

Create an idea gift exchange. It's always easier to solve someone else's problem. Have people generate ideas for each other's opportunities, projects, or problems.

Hold a "Reality Show Idea Fair" during which employees put on performances and demonstrations of how their ideas would work in real life.

Show an innovation video on Friday afternoon, complete with popcorn and sodas. Discuss the video afterward.

Identify some successful innovators in the organization or from the community and ask them to make a presentation about innovation at a brown-bag lunch.

Create a "Featured Customer" series of brown-bag lunches to help people understand customers more fully. Ask customers or people who have regular and close contact with them to make the presentations.

Create an innovation Website and publish stories of success and failure from articles and books, and publish internal and external examples of best practices.

continued on next page

Handout 11–10, continued
Improving Innovation Ideas

Invite people to join a Trend Search. Have them spend two weeks looking at everything they can find—magazines, books, papers, movies, the Web—and talking to people about what's new in the world. Ask them to come together and discuss their findings at the end of the two weeks.	Cross-fertilize by forming triads across business units or departments and talking about problems and opportunities to see what new thinking arises. Become more familiar with company strategy. Arrange an open session and ask a senior executive to discuss strategy and how it relates to innovation.	Identify subject matter experts who are visiting the organization and ask them to make presentations on their areas of interest at sessions open to everyone.

Handout 11–11
Innovation Criteria Grid

When an organization becomes adept at identifying possibilities and generating new ideas, the challenge shifts to evaluating those possibilities and ideas. This often turns out to be the most confounding aspect of the innovation process. Too often, people fall in love with ideas or potential projects, or they respond to a need of the moment and launch the wrong project at the wrong time.

Many experts say that 90 percent of all projects fail, most because they should not have begun in the first place. The Innovation Criteria Grid helps you think through the evaluation process to make sure you're working with concepts that have a reasonable chance of succeeding.

Setting evaluation criteria is critical to prioritizing possibilities. However, criteria differ depending on the project type, the organization's objectives, and the market. For example, the criteria for a project designed to cut costs differ from those of a radical innovation project. So first you must categorize the project. The Innovation Criteria Grid offers three basic categories of innovation based on the intended outcome:

1. **Transform.** This category includes new products, services, or processes that dramatically change everything, including the target market and value proposition. *Example:* cell phones.

2. **Evolve.** These possibilities can lead to distinctly new and better products, services, or processes and should create new value for customers and the organization. *Example:* wireless Internet access for cell phones or video phones.

3. **Improve.** These projects are designed to cut costs, improve what already exists, or extend current product or service lines. *Example:* customizable cell phone facecovers.

When you have identified the category of the innovation you are seeking, go to the Criteria Grid that is related to that category and rate each factor. What's important about the grid process is that it demands thinking about specific factors for success. This can be done individually by each team member. Teams should then gather and discuss the ratings given. Or the group might discuss each factor to arrive at a consensus rating. The purpose of the grid is to stimulate a broad conversation about the risks and rewards of the project. Each grid presented here includes two blank lines so that you can add criteria that are appropriate for your specific possibility.

The Innovation Criteria Grid ratings are not intended to be "go/no go" decision points. They should stimulate conversation about how to overcome weak points and how to provide a rough gauge of the relative strengths of competing projects.

continued on next page

Handout 11–11, continued

Innovation Criteria Grid

Here are the steps for using the Innovation Criteria Grid:

1. **Identify criteria.** Internal process criteria will differ from criteria for new products or services to be sold to customers. Make the criteria relevant to the project.

2. **Create an appropriate criteria grid form.** Examples are given in this handout, but you should adapt the grid to your own specific situation.

3. **Rate each criterion,** either individually or as a group.

4. **Discuss** ways to improve weak factors.

5. **Compare competing projects.** On the next several pages we've provided examples of grids for each category of innovation—transformative, evolutionary, and improvement-oriented. They're intended to get you started on creating a grid that suits your unique project or concept.

Again, remember that the purpose of this exercise is not to make a go/no go decision, but to make the concept stronger. If you were just starting to develop a concept, this evaluation might stimulate conversation about sharing risk through alliances and thinking more about the value to customers and how it would benefit various types of users.

continued on next page

Example of a Transform Innovation Criteria Grid

Transform Innovation: New products, services, or processes that dramatically change everything including the value proposition.

Instructions: The criteria are listed in the first column of the grid. The possible ratings (1–5) are defined in the next five columns. Select the rating that best describes your concept for each criterion and write it in the last column.

CRITERION	1	2	3	4	5	RATING
New market	No; current market only	Some expansion potential	Small segment of new market	Major segment of new market	Completely new, large market	
Uniqueness	Many similar options	A few similar options	Somewhat unique	Unique in many ways	Nothing like it in the market	
Transformative benefits*	Little improvement	Some improvement in one benefit	Definite improvement in one benefit	Dramatic improvement in one benefit	Dramatic improvement in one benefit	
Value for customer	Little or no new value	Some new value	Visible increase in value	Significant increase in value	Wow!	
Value for organization	Hard to identify value	New capacities	Offers entry to new market	Major player in large market	Own a huge, new, profitable market	
Fits strategy	Not at all	Slightly	Moderately	Closely	Expands strategy	
Probability of success	High probability of failure	Long shot	50–50	Probable success	Looks like a sure thing	

continued on next page

Example of a Transform Innovation Criteria Grid, continued

Transform Innovation: New products, services, or processes that dramatically change everything including the value proposition.

Instructions: The criteria are listed in the first column of the grid. The possible ratings (1–5) are defined in the next five columns. Select the rating that best describes your concept for each criterion and write it in the last column.

CRITERION	1	2	3	4	5	RATING
Investment risk	We're betting the farm	Would crowd out most other possibilities	Major capital budget item	Within business-unit approval guidelines	Cheap; no-brainer	
Ready availability of know-how	Not at all	Uncertain	Maybe	Probably	Definitely	
Partner/alliance possibilities	None	Perhaps	Some	Probably	Definitely	

*Radical innovations generally offer dramatic improvements in one or more transformative benefits, such as size, speed, convenience, durability, fuel efficiency, safety, quality, price, dependability, ease of use, distribution, or fun.

Note: Review the criteria from the Improvement-oriented Innovation Criteria Grid and add to this grid any that are appropriate for this project.

continued on next page

Example of an Evolve Innovation Criteria Grid

Evolve Innovation: Distinctly new and better products, services, or processes that create value.

Instructions: The criteria are listed in the first column of the grid. The possible ratings (1–5) are defined in the next five columns. Select the rating that best describes your concept for each criterion and write it in the last column.

CRITERION	1	2	3	4	5	RATING
Uniqueness	Many similar options	A few similar options	Somewhat unique	Unique in many ways	Nothing similar in the market	
Market potential	None	Small	Average	Large	Huge	
Fits strategy	Not at all	Slightly	Moderately	Closely	Completely	
Value for customer	None	Some	Average	Significant	High	
Value for organization	None	Some	Average	Significant	High	
Simplicity of concept	Complex and arcane	High level of education required	Some education required	Understandable by most people	Easily understood by all	
Implementation difficulty	Extremely difficult	Very difficult	Moderately difficult	Somewhat easy	Easy	
Implementation speed	Far in the future	Lengthy	Moderate	Fairly quick	Almost instant	

continued on next page

Example of an Evolve Innovation Criteria Grid, continued

Evolve Innovation: Distinctly new and better products, services, or processes that create value.

Instructions: The criteria are listed in the first column of the grid. The possible ratings (1–5) are defined in the next five columns. Select the rating that best describes your concept for each criterion and write it in the last column.

CRITERION	1	2	3	4	5	RATING
Implementation cost	Budget breaker	Would put all eggs in this basket	Major expense that requires many approvals	Within approval guidelines of business unit	Cheap; no-brainer	
Ready availability of know-how	Not at all	Uncertain	Maybe	Probably	Definitely	

Note: Review the criteria from the Improvement-oriented Innovation Criteria Grid and add to this grid any that are appropriate for this project.

continued on next page

Example of an Improve Innovation *Criteria Grid*

Improve Innovation: Improvements in what already exists, cost cutting, or line extensions.

Instructions: The criteria are listed in the first column of the grid. The possible ratings (1–5) are defined in the next five columns. Select the rating that best describes your concept for each criterion and write it in the last column.

CRITERIA	1	2	3	4	5	RATING
Implementation difficulty	Extremely difficult	Very difficult	Moderately difficult	Somewhat easy	Easy	
Implementation speed	Far in the future	Lengthy	Moderate	Fairly quick	Almost instant	
Saves money	None	Some	Moderate amount	Significant amount	Big money	
Return-on-investment	Significantly below threshold	Somewhat below threshold	Meets threshold	Somewhat above threshold	Significantly above threshold	
Easily understood	New capabilities needed	Lots of training needed	Some training needed	Some review needed	Yes	
Fits strategy	Not at all	Slightly	Moderately	Pretty well	Completely	
New resources required	Lots and expensive	Significant amount	Some	Not many	None	
Compatible with current systems and initiatives	No	Significant adjustments required	Moderate adjustments required	Minor adjustments required	Yes	

continued on next page

Example of an Improve Innovation Criteria Grid, continued

Improve Innovation: Improvements in what already exists, cost cutting, or line extensions.

Instructions: The criteria are listed in the first column of the grid. The possible ratings (1–5) are defined in the next five columns. Select the rating that best describes your concept for each criterion and write it in the last column.

CRITERIA	1	2	3	4	5	RATING
Speeds up processes	No	Some	Moderately	Significantly	Extremely	
Meets legal and ethical requirements	No	Many problems to fix	Some problems to fix	Problems easily fixed	Yes	
Easily managed	Many complications and unknowns	Highly complex	Significant uncertainties	Some uncertainties	Piece of cake	
Fits culture	Not at all	Slightly	Moderately	Mostly	Yes	
Environmentally sound	Probably not	With more work and money	Some problems to fix	Problems easily fixed	Yes	
Ready availability of know-how	Not at all	Uncertain	Maybe	Probably	Definitely	

Handout 11-12
Contemplation Matrix

Sharing ideas, insights, and lessons learned is a fundamental skill for innovation organizations, but it may be the hardest skill to develop and maintain. The pressure to deliver more with less makes people loath to stop and collect information so that it can be shared. Additionally, few organizations actually recognize or reward the effort of collecting and sharing information.

But there are some exceptions. For example, the Neenan Company, a unique and innovative construction firm in Fort Collins, Colorado, has as part of its employee evaluation program a requirement for a Learning and Sharing Contract. Annually employees commit to what they are going to learn and what they are willing to teach during the year.

There are many different types of information that should be shared and many ways to share it. The Contemplation Matrix offers you a tool for thinking of ways to promote contemplation that work specifically for your organization.

Contemplation Criteria

For a contemplation process to work well it should meet the following three simple criteria. It should be

1. **Open.** As many people as reasonable and possible should have access to the information offered, both in submitting it and in accessing it.

2. **Relevant.** The information should be fresh, pertinent, and not readily available in standard places.

3. **Modifiable.** Because new information has a way of changing, it should be easy to amend as new data are processed.

Use the Contemplation Matrix Worksheet included here to generate ideas for collecting and sharing information. For each type of information enumerated vertically in the left-hand column, think of ways you could use the transmission mechanisms described at the tops of the other columns. List as many as possible in each area. Try to use the lowest possible level of technology in the beginning. One very effective contemplation process involves creating communities of practice that meet on a regular basis to share learnings and new information.

continued on next page

Contemplation Matrix Worksheet

Instructions: Use this matrix to record ways you could share the types of information listed in the left-hand column by using the transmission methods described across the tops of the other columns.

TYPE OF INFORMATION TO COLLECT/SHARE	EMAIL OR WEBSITE	IN-PERSON MEETINGS OR TRAININGS	TELEPHONE CONFERENCE OR VOICE MAIL	DATABASE SYSTEMS— KNOWLEDGE MANAGEMENT OR IDEA MANAGEMENT	VIDEO, CD, GRAFFITI WALLS, OR OTHER
Project lessons					
Insights					
Concerns					
Ideas					
Tools and techniques					
New data regarding customers, competitors, supplies, trends, technologies					
Competitor information					

Handout 11–13
Creativity Made Simple: SWAMI SOARS!

Creativity can seem like magic...and it is...but it also can be clarified by understanding its underlying phases and principles and by grasping one very important rule.

Two Phases of Creativity

The two phases of creativity are *divergence* and *convergence.* Divergence is the stimulation of new thinking by diversifying and exploring. Convergence involves refining and choosing the best possibilities. Each phase has a series of five operating principles that happen to fit neatly into the mnemonic device *SWAMI SOARS!* (If you hate clever mnemonics, feel free to ignore it.)

One Rule of Creativity

Separate the two phases. Trying to diverge and converge at the same time makes people crazy and sucks the juice out of the creative process, leaving you with pale, lifeless ideas.

Divergence Processes: SWAMI

Although there are hundreds of divergence techniques, they basically relate to five simple processes. When you understand these processes you can easily add to your divergence toolkit without feeling overwhelmed.

The job of all divergence tools is to stimulate new thinking. Here are the five basic action processes (stated as verbs) inherent in all these tools:

1. **Suppose.** Putting yourself in imaginary situations switches on new ways of thinking. For example, if you were from Mars, what would this problem look like? If you were six years old or three feet tall, what would the future look like to you? If you could smash all the assumptions around this issue, what would happen? A useful tool for this process is creating "future stories" in which you think of headlines that you would like to see and then make up a story about how those headlines came to be.

2. **Wander.** Wandering through new territory with an open mind scoops up new connections and links. For instance, you can wander through hardware or antique stores, new magazines or conferences, random images or analogies from nature. A helpful tool here is to use random images taken from magazines and other sources, photographs, or postcards to stimulate thinking about whatever issue you are working on.

3. **Associate.** Deliberately create new links between objects, ideas, events, people, or processes. As you link things together that normally are not connected, you begin to see new relationships and new possibilities. Metaphorical thinking is a helpful tool here because you use the qualities of one object to think about another. For instance, if you're trying to create better customer service, you might think about the qualities

continued on next page

---

of a rubber ball...it's round and smooth, it bounces and is resilient, it isn't easily damaged, and it's fun to play with. Then you would examine each of those qualities to see what ideas they might stimulate around customer service.

4. **Morph.** Change various aspects of the situation; make the familiar strange and the strange familiar. Brainwriting is a very simple tool for incorporating the process of morphing and building on other ideas. The Brainwriting worksheet has six rows and three columns of empty boxes. Each person in the brainstorming session writes three ideas in one row of boxes on one worksheet and then passes the sheet to another person. Everyone can read the ideas of others and build on them or use them to stimulate new ideas. The exercise is repeated until all the sheets are filled. (See Handout 11–7 for BrainwritingPlus worksheets.)

5. **Inquire.** Questions create openings. A great question can unravel a mystery like a kitten batting a ball of twine. Finding those great questions that open minds and the secrets of the universe is a learned skill based on some simple principles and practice. One of the best questions to use to open up new possibilities is "Wouldn't it be great if...?" Try opening a brainstorming session by having everyone think of 10 ways to complete that question.

Convergence Processes: SOARS

There are almost as many convergence techniques as there are divergence ones, but again they relate to five basic processes. Convergence tools make sense of what is often an overwhelming number of possibilities, and narrow the range of choices in order to make an intelligent decision. Here are the five action processes (again stated as verbs) to which all convergence tools relate :

1. **Sort.** To make sense of what is often hundreds of possibilities, group them into meaningful categories. Categories might be related to time, feasibility, market demand, availability of resources, type of possibility, or any other category that would bring order out of the chaos. A simple tool is a three-color sort using the widely understood color coding of green-yellow-red. In this tool green represents ideas that clearly fit with your criteria, yellow is for ideas that have some fit but probably need further thought, and red identifies ideas that do not fit the criteria.

2. **Order.** Possibilities within viable categories can be ranked against preestablished criteria to create an order of preference. Using a simple quadrant chart incorporating two important criteria (such as cost and doability) is a powerful way to see which ideas best fit the criteria.

continued on next page

Handout 11–13, continued
Creativity Made Simple: SWAMI SOARS!

3. **Adapt.** When likely possibilities have been identified they can be expanded and adapted to create even better ideas. Take Away is one simple tool for adapting ideas. To use the tool, identify critical components of an idea and then take one component away and see what you would have to do if that component wasn't available or didn't exist. For example, if you didn't have access to electricity you might start thinking about phones that didn't have to be plugged in.

4. **Refine.** The weak spots and potential failure points need to be identified for all likely possibilities, and then the ideas must be bullet-proofed. To bullet-proof an idea, first think of all the ways it could fail or what external events might create a disaster or who might say "no." Then begin to brainstorm ways to avoid possible problems.

5. **Select.** Ideas are only ideas until they are implemented, but implementation requires that someone take ownership. Getting the right people to take ownership of the idea is a critical piece of the process. Dot Voting is one of the easiest techniques for selecting ideas. Make all of the choices available and give each participant in the process a certain number of dots to vote. If you have established the criteria in advance this process can be very effective for selecting the best ideas and getting buy-in from people as they see that certain concepts match the criteria more than others. (See Handout 11–14 for more information.)

Handout 11–14

Dot Voting with a Difference

Imagine this situation: You've been in an ideation session for half a day and the walls of the room are covered with hundreds of sticky notes. You know that most of the ideas are just fodder, but within this chaos there are undoubtedly some gems. How do you make a decision? One of the easiest and most acceptable ways is dot voting, but there's one step that most people miss—the step that makes this a far more powerful process—identifying criteria. Here's how dot voting with a difference works:

Step 1.   **Step back from the ideas** and take a clean piece of flipchart paper.

Step 2.   **Identify criteria.** Brainstorm the criteria for evaluating an idea or solution. You might say, "A good idea or solution would have the following characteristics:...." Perhaps there's a budget constraint or a time deadline; maybe specific materials are needed or it has to appeal to a certain person or group of customers; possibly it has to be no bigger than a deck of cards, or ...well, you get the idea.

Step 3.   **Prioritize.** When you have the list of criteria (which probably won't be more than 5 to 10 items), try to reach consensus on the priority of the criteria. If this is too difficult you may need to dot-vote the criteria, according to the process in the next step.

Step 4.   **Vote.** Now that everyone has the decision criteria in mind, have them use a colored marker that will show up easily and give them three to five votes each. People mark their votes by making a visible dot on whatever ideas they choose.

Step 5.   **Rearrange the ideas** so that those with the dots are grouped together, ranked from most dots to least.

Step 6.   **Discuss.** Talk about the idea(s) that received the most votes and see if there is a general level of comfort with taking one or more of those ideas to the next step.

Step 7.   **Recognize orphans.** Before ending the session ask everyone to review the undotted ideas one more time to see if there are any "orphans" there that someone thinks should be given a home somewhere.

Step 8.   **Plan next steps.** Decide what should happen next and how to capture the ideas so you can throw away the mountain of sticky notes.

Handout 11–15

Dimensions of the InnovationDNA Model

The InnovationDNA model presents a framework of the principles needed to create an "innovation organization."

◆ **Context**—*formed by the interactions between the organization and the outside world.* Nothing so important as organizational innovation happens in a vacuum. Although it is obvious that customers, suppliers, competitors, and the economy affect us daily, we also periodically interact with government, world events, communities, and families. All of these interactions form the context for all business activities, including innovation.

◆ **Culture**—*the backdrop for all the activities of an organization and the "playing field" for innovation.* Whereas innovation is "for the sake of" creating value for customers or a lofty vision, the organization must be fertile for the seeds of ideas and solutions to grow. An environment that is empowering and flexible, that welcomes ideas and tolerates risk, that celebrates success, fosters synergy, and encourages fun is crucial. Creating such a climate also may be the biggest challenge facing any organization that wishes to be more innovative. We see four main components of an organization's culture that provide the climate for innovation to occur. Those components are leadership, people, basic values, and innovation values.

1. **Leadership**—*the ability to see the possibilities of the future.* Strategies are put into place because leaders can envision a bright future and identify opportunities that can pave the path to success. Engaging the hearts of people and providing the necessary support are necessary to make the vision a reality.

2. **People**—*the heart and soul of innovation.* Nothing happens without people. Every organization has a "personality" that comes from its collective and shared beliefs, attitudes, and behaviors and from the relationships among its people.

3. **Basic Values**—*heartfelt principles that define an organization.* Basic values, such as learning, commitment, inclusiveness, and contribution, are the kinds of principles that help an organization hold its shape in the frantic pace of global business. They are the backbone for decisions and the foundation for shaping strategic alliances.

4. **Innovation Values**—*what makes the impossible possible.* Beyond basic values there are some drivers that can transform the mundane into the compelling and an ordinary project into a stellar new business. Freedom, intuition, and synergy are just a few of the ideals that create the magic in innovative organizations.

continued on next page

The DNA concept came from the work of the Founding Fellowship class of Innovation University. We continue to study and update the model.

Handout 11–15, continued
Dimensions of the InnovationDNA Model

- **Entryways to Innovation . . . Ideas, Change, Passion, and Trends**—*the impetus to rock the boat.*

- **Outcomes of Innovation . . . Renewal, Change, Reinvention, and Trends**—*fuel for the next cycle.*

The Operational Elements of the Innovation DNA—a Roadmap

It is useful to view the operational elements depicted on the helix as a roadmap, beginning at the bottom portal and moving upward. Here are brief descriptions of the model's concepts.

- **Challenge**—Innovating, by definition, means doing things differently, exploring new territory, and taking risks. However, there has to be a reason for rocking the boat, and that reason is the *vision* of what could be . . . the challenge. The bigger the challenge and the commitment to it, the more energy the innovation efforts will have. Whether it is today's survival or a lofty vision that benefits all of humankind, superb innovation is driven by challenges that touch people's hearts.

- **Customer Focus**—All innovation should be focused on creating *value* for the customer, whether that customer is internal or external. Interacting with customers and understanding their needs are the best means of stimulating new possibilities and the motivation for implementing them. A constant, almost involuntary, stream of ideas and innovation is created when everyone in an organization can identify with their customer(s).

- **Creativity**—Everything starts from an idea, and the best way to get a great idea is to generate a lot of possibilities. Although every person is creative by nature, the skill to develop a lot of ideas and to connect diverse concepts can be enhanced through training and exercise. It is up to leadership to foster a climate that encourages "blue-sky" thinking and to offer direction and *stimuli* to spur creativity. It is up to individuals to embrace challenges and give themselves permission to push the boundaries of their thinking.

- **Communication**—Open communication of information, ideas, and feelings is the lifeblood of innovation. Both infrastructure and advocacy must exist in an organizational system to promote the free flow of information. Leadership must model the practices and behaviors that will encourage the sharing of information and, more critical, the sharing of thinking. Organizations that restrict communication and fail to "think together" risk disaster.

- **Collaboration**—Innovation is a group process. It feeds on interaction, information, and the power of *teams.* It is stifled by restrictive structures, policies, and practices, as well as incentive systems that reward only individual efforts. Multilevel and cross-functional project and ad hoc teams bring diversity—the broadest perspectives, the most ideas, and the greatest abilities to implement—to any innovation effort.

continued on next page

Handout 11–15, continued
Dimensions of the InnovationDNA Model

◆ **Completion**—Moving new ideas forward into reality means crossing the threshold from creativity to innovation, and the exploration or experimentation with a variety of alternatives will yield superior outcomes. Innovations result from projects that are successfully realized through excellent, defined processes and strong implementation skills—decision making, delegating, scheduling, monitoring, and feedback. And when projects are completed, they should be celebrated.

◆ **Contemplation**—Making objective *assessments* of the outcomes and costs of new projects is essential. Gleaning the *lessons learned* from both fruitful and failed projects adds muscle to the cycle of success. This practice of review and integration is perhaps the most neglected component of innovation. When adopted in a disciplined approach, it adds invaluably to organization wisdom.

Handout 11–16

PIC Gap Analysis

Perform Self-Assessment: Read each competency and mark an "A" in the column that reflects the knowledge/behavior you currently demonstrate.

Identify Goal: Next, review each item and mark a "B" in the column that is your goal for future competency.

Define Gap: Draw a line between A and B on each item to illustrate the competency gap.

Select Action: Using the PIC Personal Action Worksheet (Handout 11–17), select two to three items that you would like to improve on and create your learning plan.

Reassess Yourself: Assess your progress monthly.

Rating Key

◆ **Unknowing:** This is new thinking to me.

◆ **Novice:** I understand and practice this behavior about 10 percent of the time.

◆ **Advanced Beginner:** I'm getting the hang of it and practice this behavior 10–25 percent of the time.

◆ **Competent:** I really get it and demonstrate this behavior 25–50 percent of the time.

◆ **Proficient:** I model this behavior more than 50 percent of the time and am beginning to mentor others.

◆ **Master:** I embody this behavior more than 90 percent of time and am evolving higher standards.

continued on next page

Handout 11–16, continued

PIC Gap Analysis

	UNKNOWING	NOVICE	ADVANCED BEGINNER	COMPETENT	PROFICIENT	MASTER
A. Commits to the exploration and development of new possibilities						
1. Looks for "a better way" and challenges the conventional						
2. Actively explores uncharted territory						
3. Embraces diversity as a vital source of new perspectives and possibilities						
4. Facilitates development of ideas into project plans						
B. Seeks out and creates new connections between unrelated concepts						
5. Regularly reads the world for new trends, technologies, ideas, and information						
6. Thinks with the whole brain and all the senses						
7. Remains open-minded and searches for opposites, anomalies, and outliers						
8. Finds or creates new combinations and synergies						

continued on next page

Handout 11–16, continued

PIC Gap Analysis

	UNKNOWING	NOVICE	ADVANCED BEGINNER	COMPETENT	PROFICIENT	MASTER
C. Commits to the creation of customer value						
9. Understands customer needs, goals, and paradigms						
10. Understands the strategic context and aims for win–win situations						
11. Strives to deliver more with less, and to do it elegantly						
D. Integrates the specific business focus with the process of innovation						
12. Understands the current art, science, and language of the business area						
13. Knows the background and context well enough to recognize ideas that are innovations						
14. Masters the basic tools and methods in the area of exploration						
15. Understands the system of innovation and allows time for each step of the process						
E. Builds alignment around new possibilities						
16. Paints the WOW picture of the future						
17. Relates new ideas to existing business strategies and objectives						
18. Speaks to the styles and concerns of each stakeholder						
19. Honors ideas regardless of origin						
F. Cultivates genuine relationships						
20. Builds trust implicitly and explicitly						

continued on next page

Handout 11–16, continued
PIC Gap Analysis

	UNKNOWING	NOVICE	ADVANCED BEGINNER	COMPETENT	PROFICIENT	MASTER
21. Respects rights and opinions of others						
22. Expresses appreciation and honest concerns						
23. Values the intent and context of a relationship						
G. Embraces appropriate risk taking						
24. Takes calculated and appropriate risks to advance ideas						
25. Is able to predict and track existing and emerging risks						
26. Finds ways to ameliorate risks						
27. Communicates risks appropriately						
H. Manages innovation projects effectively						
28. Employs tools, processes, and techniques flexibly and effectively						
29. Honors and manages requests, offers, and promises						
30. Focuses on the germane issues and juggles priorities						
31. Scans the business climate to optimize timing for actions						
32. Guides effective decision making						
33. Elicits the agreement of "done"						

continued on next page

Handout 11–16, continued

PIC Gap Analysis

	UNKNOWING	NOVICE	ADVANCED BEGINNER	COMPETENT	PROFICIENT	MASTER
I. Learns relentlessly						
34. Cultivates an internal state of curiosity						
35. Seeks information and feedback; actively asks questions						
36. Assesses failures and successes to find lessons						
37. Challenges own assumptions						
38. Acknowledges other world views						

Handout 11–17
PIC Personal Action Worksheet

Name _____

Date _____

Step 1: Select two to three Personal Innovation Competencies to build on and record them here.

Step 2: Choose one to three tools to learn or practices and behaviors to adopt; record them here.

Step 3: Choose your metrics for determining progress and success; record metrics and monthly goals.

Step 4: Monitor your progress monthly.

Competency #1: _____

IMPROVEMENT ACTIVITY	METRIC	START DATE	MONTH 1 GOAL	OUTCOME	MONTH 2 GOAL	OUTCOME	MONTH 3 GOAL	OUTCOME

continued on next page

Handout 11–17, continued
PIC Personal Action Worksheet

Competency #2: _____

IMPROVEMENT ACTIVITY	METRIC	START DATE	MONTH 1 GOAL	OUTCOME	MONTH 2 GOAL	OUTCOME	MONTH 3 GOAL	OUTCOME

Competency #3: _____

IMPROVEMENT ACTIVITY	METRIC	START DATE	MONTH 1 GOAL	OUTCOME	MONTH 2 GOAL	OUTCOME	MONTH 3 GOAL	OUTCOME

Handout 11–18
PIC Discussion Guide

Category A—Commits to the exploration and development of new possibilities

Step 1: *Have someone read aloud the following background of this category. (If in pairs, you may prefer to read silently together.)*

The first competency for innovation is defined by openness, exploration, and the abilities to envision and promote new possibilities. By its very nature innovation seeks a better way. Innovators are like explorers: They push forward into uncharted territory, sometimes just to find out what's there. They open themselves to ideas that are unfamiliar and perhaps disconcerting.

Innovation is as much a mindset as it is tools and techniques. The mindset of innovation is to look for new and better solutions. Instead of stopping at the first right answer, innovators continue to ask "How else could we do this?" or "What would make it even better?"

Deliberately exploring uncharted territory can be as simple as reading magazines and newspapers outside of your normal realm of interest; talking to people with different perspectives and backgrounds; attending conferences on topics you are completely unfamiliar with; and traveling through new countries, neighborhoods or markets. Being inquisitive, discovering what you ***don't*** know and stimulating others' thinking are all hallmarks of an innovator.

Master innovators are also leaders. They help those around them to envision new possibilities and frontiers, thereby engaging their hearts and minds for the pursuit of innovation.

Step 2: *Discuss the following questions, one for each of the four behaviors that characterize this competency. Take turns capturing the key points discussed for each question because you will be asked to present these points to the larger group.*

- ◆ ***Behavior 1. Looking for a better way; challenging convention:*** In your organization what are the ways that people can challenge the status quo? How are ideas for a "better way" most productively channeled?
- ◆ ***Behavior 2. Actively exploring uncharted territory:*** What would be uncharted territory for your organization? What are ways that new frontiers could be discovered and explored?
- ◆ ***Behavior 3. Embracing diversity:*** What kinds of diversity exist in your organization. How might they be tapped for ideas?
- ◆ ***Behavior 4. Facilitating new challenges:*** What was a challenge put forth in your organization that captured your interest and spurred your imagination? What kind of challenge could you offer to stimulate others' energies?

continued on next page

Handout 11–18, continued

PIC Discussion Guide

Category B: Seeks out and creates new connections between unrelated concepts

Step 1: *Have someone read aloud the following background of this category. (If in pairs, you may prefer to read silently together.)*

There will always be original ideas generated and new technologies developed, but most money is made by improving ideas and finding new combinations of previously unrelated concepts. This is the essence of creative thinking. The keys to discovering these recombinations include constant scanning of what's going on in the world, using whole-brain thinking, investigating anomalies, and experimenting.

Innovation includes a process of opening up to the world, allowing new information from a wide variety of sources to mix and form new patterns. To allow this free flow of information we need to understand our own thinking style, how others think, and ways to stimulate creativity that maximize our exploration of new data and insights.

As we actively scan the world, we are looking for new patterns; things that look out of place; activities occurring on the fringe of different fields; and shifts in values, moral attitudes, and interests. We can playfully combine and recombine these shifting sands of change to make new connections and find synergies.

Step 2: *Discuss the following questions, one for each of the four behaviors that characterize this competency. Take turns capturing the key points discussed for each question because you will be asked to present these points to the larger group.*

- ◆ ***Behavior 1. Reading the world:*** Where can you find information about new trends or technologies? How can your organization digest and use this information?
- ◆ ***Behavior 2. Using the whole brain and all the senses:*** What words would you use to characterize how you receive and process information—are you good at analysis or synthesis of data, at organizing or intuiting?
- ◆ ***Behavior 3. Searching for anomalies:*** What are some things you've noticed lately that are inconsistent with the past? How might they change the course of your organization?
- ◆ ***Behavior 4. Creating new combinations and synergies:*** Think of two very different ideas that you've heard of recently. Try combining them—what new directions do you see?

Category C: Commits to the creation of customer value

Step 1: *Have someone read aloud the following background of this category. (If in pairs, you may prefer to read silently together.)*

The focal point of innovation is the customer, whether internal or external. Successful innovators dig deep to understand their customer's or user's most profound concerns. It is the intersection of customer needs and concerns with your organization's strategy and goals that allows for the solutions that customers value.

continued on next page

Handout 11–18, continued
PIC Discussion Guide

Innovation is people creating value by implementing new ideas. The focus on creating value distinguishes innovation from the empty process of being creative simply for the sake of creating something new. The internal or external customer and what we perceive he or she needs are the compass of innovation.

Value is determined by the customer. The innovative process is collaborative and works within a strategic context to provide valuable solutions for all stakeholders. It is also a synergistic process that finds ways to deliver results that exceed customer expectations.

Step 2: *Discuss the following questions, one for each of the three behaviors that characterize this competency. Take turns capturing the key points discussed for each question because you will be asked to present these points to the larger group.*

- *Behavior 1. Understanding customers:* How can you learn more about and better understand your internal and external customers?
- *Behavior 2. Understanding strategy and win–win:* What are ways to achieve your organization's goals that will allow you and your internal and external customers to win?
- *Behavior 3. Doing more with less to exceed customer expectations:* In what ways could you create more by doing less and yet delight your customers (internal or external)?

Category D: Integrates business focus with the process of innovation

Step 1: *Have someone read aloud the following background of this category. (If in pairs, you may prefer to read silently together.)*

Great innovators are also good business people. They keep pace with their industry and are aware of what others are doing. They are masters of the tools, methods, and practices that represent their industry standard, and they are skillful at the process of innovation. Part of innovation is constantly sharpening of business acumen and expertise in one's own field. The other part is mastery of the practices and tools of innovation.

Ideas often show up unexpectedly and so there is a tendency to believe that creative thinking is uncontrollable. Although it cannot truly be "controlled," it can be enhanced and strengthened. The formula is reliable:

*Passionate Focus + Abundant Information + Diverse Thinkers
+ Idea Stimulators = A Wealth of Ideas*

Innovation takes time and involves a rigorous process. It takes time to align around a challenge, gather information, and think together. It takes discipline to reflect on and refine ideas, work collaboratively to implement them, and learn lessons along the way. It's a process that involves the hearts and minds of many people. There is no magic "innovation" machine that pops out breakthrough solutions complete with nice, neat, cost-justified printouts at the end.

continued on next page

Handout 11–18, continued
PIC Discussion Guide

Step 2: *Discuss the following questions, one for each of the four behaviors that characterize this competency. Take turns capturing the key points discussed for each question because you will be asked to present these points to the larger group.*

- *Behavior 1. Understanding the states of the art and science of the field:* What are the ways you stay current in your functional field and your industry?

- *Behavior 2. Being able to recognize what is novel or innovative in your field or industry:* What are some recent innovations in your industry or functional field and how have they affected your thinking?

- *Behavior 3. Mastering the tools and methodologies of your field or industry:* What tools and skills would help you become an innovation master in your field or industry?

- *Behavior 4. Understanding and executing the innovation process:* With your skills and talents, what parts of the innovation process should you focus on to become a master innovator?

Category E: Builds alignment around new possibilities

Step 1: *Have someone read aloud the following background of this category. (If in pairs, you may prefer to read silently together.)*

Innovation starts with an idea, and ideas need champions to nurture and promote them. Competent innovators understand stakeholder concerns and can connect the dots between vision and the ideas that will enable the vision. They paint compelling pictures of the future, embrace the ideas of others, and facilitate communication and alignment around ideas and actions.

New ideas seldom sell themselves into implementation. Even the Post-It! almost died many times along the way and only became a mega-hit because of the persistence and passion of many people who saw its potential.

It's critical to understand the deep concerns of your audience and to speak their language. If you are presenting an idea to a group of engineers, it should look dramatically different than a presentation to an ad agency.

Innovators know that ideas can come from the most unlikely places so they listen carefully to ideas even when they are presented in an unfamiliar or inelegant fashion. They rigorously resist the "Not Invented Here" syndrome.

Step 2: *Discuss the following questions, one for each of the four behaviors that characterize this competency. Take turns capturing the key points discussed for each question because you will be asked to present these points to the larger group.*

- *Behavior 1. Painting the WOW picture:* What are some elements of a future picture that would wow people in your organization?

continued on next page

Handout 11–18, continued
PIC Discussion Guide

- **Behavior 2. Connecting ideas and strategy:** What strategies in your organization may require new ideas for successful execution?
- **Behavior 3. Addressing stakeholders' concerns and styles:** How do you learn about the concerns of all the stakeholders?
- **Behavior 4. Welcoming and honoring ideas:** What are ways to ensure that everyone's ideas are solicited and acknowledged?

Category F: Cultivates genuine relationships

Step 1: *Have someone read aloud the following background of this category. (If in pairs, you may prefer to read silently together.)*

Innovation requires trust and collaboration because no idea can flourish without a team effort. To be an effective collaborator you must honor others' opinions and be sincere, reliable, and compassionately honest. Building productive relationships with colleagues is hard work, but it is the foundation for tremendous success and fulfillment.

Innovation is a risky adventure, one people do not take lightly. Successful innovators must know whether they can trust the system not to punish them for taking appropriate risks. They must also trust colleagues not to ridicule them for half-baked or seemingly silly ideas. The more fear is removed from an organization, the more people will feel free to open up, share ideas, and try new things. Although not all relationships are equal, among teammates who develop a high level of trust there is opportunity for superior collaboration and remarkable outcomes.

Beyond trust, collaborative relationships require respect—for the opinions and concerns of everyone. Some of the best ideas may come from the most unlikely sources throughout the organization. And without the bedrock of relationships that are grounded in honesty, sincere appreciation, and respect for each other's boundaries, serious insights and deep concerns may never come to light.

Step 2: *Discuss the following questions, one for each of the four behaviors that characterize this competency. Take turns capturing the key points discussed for each question because you will be asked to present these points to the larger group.*

- **Behavior 1. Building trust:** In what ways do people build trust between and among themselves? What are some of the causes of distrust among co-workers?
- **Behavior 2. Respecting others:** How do people in your organization demonstrate that they honor differing perspectives or minority opinions?
- **Behavior 3. Expressing appreciation and honest concerns:** If you had a serious concern today, how would you go about making it known and what is your expectation of the response?
- **Behavior 4. Valuing relationship intent and context:** How would you describe the different kinds of relationships you have with various people in the organization?

continued on next page

Handout 11–18, *continued*

PIC Discussion Guide

Category G: Embraces appropriate risk taking

Step 1: *Have someone read aloud the following background of this category. (If in pairs, you may prefer to read silently together.)*

Because innovation, by definition, is doing something that has not been done before, its success is uncertain. Therefore, risk is a requirement of innovation. Many organizations have been risk averse for decades, and now people are being asked to take risks in order to innovate. It's a tricky transition. Organizations that punish people who support the wrong idea will soon find the flow of ideas drying up. Likewise, people who never stick their necks out for new ideas may find themselves in pale and lackluster careers.

Knowing the difference between calculated risk and risky business is paramount in innovation. Learning how to advance ideas appropriately can mitigate but not eliminate the risk involved. Many ideas embody risk—some in the mere advancement, others in the execution.

The first step is to understand what the risk represents to stakeholders—is it loss of revenue or profit, is it retribution or the loss of career advancement, is it the danger of bankruptcy? Weighing the risk against potential rewards is the daily work of some financial heads in your organization. In an open environment innovators and their managers can work collaboratively to predict, track, and manage the risks that innovation presents.

Step 2: *Discuss the following questions, one for each of the four behaviors that characterize this competency. Take turns capturing the key points discussed for each question because you will be asked to present these points to the larger group.*

- ◆ *Behavior 1. Taking calculated and appropriate risks to advance ideas:* Can you describe a situation in which someone in the organization took a calculated risk and succeeded? How was the risk managed?
- ◆ *Behavior 2. Predicting and tracking risk:* Can you think of a current project or initiative in the organization and can you identify some of its risks to stakeholders?
- ◆ *Behavior 3. Relieving or reducing risk:* Using the current project or initiative you described in the previous question, what are ways the stakeholders' risks could be managed?
- ◆ *Behavior 4. Effectively communicating about risk:* In this organization what are the most effective ways to communicate information and beliefs about risk and risk management?

Category H: Effectively manages innovation projects

Step 1: *Have someone read aloud the following background of this category. (If in pairs, you may prefer to read silently together.)*

continued on next page

Handout 11–18, continued

PIC Discussion Guide

Projects must often adjust over time with the changing business and economic climate. By definition, innovation projects should be flexible and follow the value chain. Effective innovators pay close attention to managing promises, juggling priorities, making decisions, and timing for actions. They leverage tools, processes, and methodologies in a conscious fashion to reach intended results.

Most successful organizations are competent in general project management, but the understanding of how to manage an *innovation* project is not always as clear. Innovation project managers must be excellent collaborators, facilitators, and synthesizers. They manage projects and the innovation *process* and help build relationships among team members. They pay attention to timing through continual scanning of the business climate and understanding of the big picture and the concerns of stakeholders.

Master innovators develop criteria in advance and make decisions in a disciplined manner. They establish metrics, track progress, and maintain timely communication with all of the people concerned, adjusting course and actions as needed. When the end is recognized, they celebrate completion, regardless of the project's outcome.

Step 2: *Discuss the following questions, one for each of the six behaviors that characterize this competency. Take turns capturing the key points discussed for each question because you will be asked to present these points to the larger group.*

- ◆ *Behavior 1. Employing tools, processes, and techniques effectively:* What tools, processes, or techniques are available in your organization to support innovation projects?
- ◆ *Behavior 2. Managing promises and priorities:* What are the key factors in effectively managing your promises or the requests made of you?
- ◆ *Behavior 3. Optimizing the timing of actions:* What are ways to determine the best timing for the implementation of new ideas?
- ◆ *Behavior 4. Guiding effective decisions:* Thinking of a decision that needs to be made soon, what are some criteria that, if applied, would lead to a sound and culturally appropriate decision?
- ◆ *Behavior 5. Monitoring progress and communicating with stakeholders:* Who might be the stakeholders for big ideas in your functional area and what metrics would those stakeholders want?
- ◆ *Behavior 6. Celebrating completion:* What are some ways to celebrate or acknowledge failure appropriately?

Category I: Learns relentlessly

Step 1: *Have someone read aloud the following background of this category. (If in pairs, you may prefer to read silently together.)*

continued on next page

Handout 11–18, continued

PIC Discussion Guide

Master innovators are curious—their endless search for what, how, and why fuels new ideas and vast possibilities. Successful innovation often requires much experimentation and leaves many failures in its wake. Innovators who seek feedback, examine the reasons behind success or failure, and challenge their own assumptions will find themselves constantly propelled forward.

Learning is an itch that is scratched by new information and new understanding. Feeding our curiosity creates a constant flow of new information that stimulates new patterns and understandings. Posing stimulating questions is a common trait of people who become experts at innovation.

Innovation projects can yield enormous knowledge for the organization if lessons are captured and shared widely—whether the project was deemed a success or a failure. Creating a forum for learning, asking questions, and giving and getting feedback is one vehicle for gaining organizational wisdom.

Breaking out of our own world view to accept other perspectives requires that we continually acknowledge and challenge our own assumptions and the assumptions of the organization. It is this constant search for data, insight, and meaning that keeps innovators on the leading edge.

Step 2: *Discuss the following questions, one for each of the five behaviors that characterize this competency. Take turns capturing the key points discussed for each question because you will be asked to present these points to the larger group.*

- ◆ *Behavior 1. Cultivating a state of curiosity:* What are you curious about? How might you cultivate similar curiosity in other things?

- ◆ *Behavior 2. Asking questions for information and feedback:* What kinds of questions could you ask, and of whom, that would help you spark ideas for innovation?

- ◆ *Behavior 3. Gleaning lessons from failure and success:* What vehicles are currently used to gather and share lessons from projects or initiatives? What are other methods that might be effective in this organization?

- ◆ *Behavior 4. Challenging assumptions:* What are some assumptions you hold that may be limiting your thinking or even your career?

- ◆ *Behavior 5. Acknowledging other world views:* Thinking of someone you respect whose perspective on an important topic is very different from yours, how has this other perspective influenced your thinking?

Handout 11–19
The Personal Innovation Competencies

Category A—Commits to the exploration and development of new possibilities

The first competency for innovation is defined by openness, exploration, and the abilities to envision and promote new possibilities. By its very nature innovation seeks a better way. Innovators are like explorers: They push forward into uncharted territory, sometimes just to find out what's there. They open themselves to ideas that are unfamiliar and perhaps disconcerting.

Innovation is as much a mindset as it is tools and techniques. The mindset of innovation is to look for new and better solutions. Instead of stopping at the first right answer, innovators continue to ask "How else could we do this?" or "What would make it even better?"

Deliberately exploring uncharted territory can be as simple as reading magazines and newspapers outside of your normal realm of interest; talking to people with different perspectives and backgrounds; attending conferences on topics you are completely unfamiliar with; and traveling through new countries, neighborhoods or markets. Being inquisitive, discovering what you *don't* know and stimulating others' thinking are all hallmarks of an innovator.

Master innovators are also leaders. They help those around them to envision new possibilities and frontiers, thereby engaging their hearts and minds for the pursuit of innovation.

Some ways to build these competencies:

- Read publications that present a broad view of the world.
- Attend conferences or workshops that are outside your field or function.
- Join an organization that thinks about the future.
- Create a list of stimulating questions.
- Create a forum for exploring unconventional ideas.
- Create a practice for challenging assumptions regularly.
- Join an organization that will stimulate your thinking and expand your horizons.
- Find ways to think with visionaries.

These are generic ideas—can you think of any more? How can you personalize these ideas?

Category B: Seeks out and creates new connections between unrelated concepts

There will always be original ideas generated and new technologies developed, but most money is made by improving ideas and finding new combinations of previously unrelated concepts. This is the essence of creative thinking. The keys to discovering these recombinations include constant scanning of what's going on in the world, using whole-brain thinking, investigating anomalies, and experimenting.

continued on next page

Handout 11–19, continued
The Personal Innovation Competencies

Innovation includes a process of opening up to the world, allowing new information from a wide variety of sources to mix and form new patterns. To allow this free flow of information we need to understand our own thinking style, how others think, and ways to stimulate creativity that maximize our exploration of new data and insights.

As we actively scan the world, we are looking for new patterns, things that look out of place, activities occurring on the fringe of different fields, and shifts in values, moral attitudes, and interests. We can playfully combine and recombine these shifting sands of change to make new connections and find synergies.

Some ways to build these competencies:

* Keep up with current events—social, political, economic, and scientific.
* Read professional publications and your industry's periodicals.
* Discover your preferred thinking style to help you determine how you best process information and how you do your best thinking.
* Create a practice to look for anomalies or outliers that could spur innovation.
* Study the perimeters of your industry for opportunities that are far from the mainstream.
* Practice putting together unrelated concepts to see what results.
* Learn some creative thinking tools that will help to combine unlikely concepts.

These are generic ideas—can you think of any more? How can you personalize these ideas?

Category C: Commits to the creation of customer value

The focal point of innovation is the customer, whether internal or external. Successful innovators dig deep to understand their customer's or user's most profound concerns. It is the intersection of customer needs and concerns with your organization's strategy and goals that allows for the solutions that customers value.

Innovation is people creating value by implementing new ideas. The focus on creating value distinguishes innovation from the empty process of being creative simply for the sake of creating something new. The internal or external customer and what we perceive he or she needs are the compass of innovation.

Value is determined by the customer. The innovative process is collaborative and works within a strategic context to provide valuable solutions for all stakeholders. It is also a synergistic process that finds ways to deliver results that exceed customer expectations.

Some ways to build these competencies:

* Create ways to observe customers.
* Create ways to talk to customers about their needs and expectations.
* Gather and study available information about your customers.

continued on next page

Handout 11–19, continued
The Personal Innovation Competencies

◆ Get to know a handful of customers and cultivate meaningful relationships.

◆ Talk to managers about your organizational strategy and how your and your function fits in it.

◆ Talk to stakeholders about their objectives.

These are generic ideas—can you think of any more? How can you personalize these ideas?

Category D: Integrates business focus with the process of innovation

Great innovators are also good business people. They keep pace with their industry and are aware of what others are doing. They are masters of the tools, methods, and practices that represent their industry standard, and they are skillful at the process of innovation. Part of innovation is constant sharpening of business acumen and expertise in one's own field. The other part is mastery of the practices and tools of innovation.

Ideas often show up unexpectedly and so there is a tendency to believe that creative thinking is uncontrollable. Although it cannot truly be "controlled," it can be enhanced and strengthened. The formula is reliable:

Passionate Focus + Abundant Information + Diverse Thinkers
+ Idea Stimulators = A Wealth of Ideas

Innovation takes time and involves a rigorous process. It takes time to align around a challenge, gather information, and think together. It takes discipline to reflect on and refine ideas, work collaboratively to implement them, and learn lessons along the way. It's a process that involves the hearts and minds of many people. There is no magic innovation machine that pops out breakthrough solutions complete with nice, neat, cost-justified printouts at the end.

Some ways to build these competencies:

◆ Attend your industry conferences.

◆ Read your industry journals.

◆ Research the history of your company and the industry.

◆ Become more familiar with your organization's strategic thinking process.

◆ Create an inventory of tools, methodologies, processes, and practices of your industry and profession.

◆ Research the innovation processes used by other organizations and industries.

These are generic ideas—can you think of any more? How can you personalize these ideas?

continued on next page

Handout 11–19, continued
The Personal Innovation Competencies

Category E: Builds alignment around new possibilities

Innovation starts with an idea, and ideas need champions to nurture and promote them. Competent innovators understand stakeholder concerns and can connect the dots between vision and the ideas that will enable the vision. They paint compelling pictures of the future, embrace the ideas of others, and facilitate communication and alignment around ideas and actions.

New ideas seldom sell themselves into implementation. Even the Post-It! almost died many times along the way and only became a mega-hit because of the persistence and passion of many people who saw its potential.

It's critical to understand the deep concerns of your audience and to speak their language. If you are presenting an idea to a group of engineers, it should look dramatically different than a presentation to an ad agency.

Innovators know that ideas can come from the most unlikely places so they listen carefully to ideas even when they are presented in an unfamiliar or inelegant fashion. They rigorously resist the "Not Invented Here" syndrome.

Some ways to build these competencies:

- Practice creating compelling stories.
- Interview organizational stakeholders to understand their objectives and underlying concerns.
- Review your company's most recent strategy document and determine how your role contributes to it.
- Look for hidden opportunities in your company strategy or industry.
- Seek ideas from colleagues.

These are generic ideas—can you think of any more? How can you personalize these ideas?

Category F: Cultivates genuine relationships

Innovation requires trust and collaboration because no idea can flourish without a team effort. To be an effective collaborator you must honor others' opinions and be sincere, reliable, and compassionately honest. Building productive relationships with colleagues is hard work, but it is the foundation for tremendous success and fulfillment.

Innovation is a risky adventure, one people do not take lightly. Successful innovators must know whether they can trust the system not to punish them for taking appropriate risks. They must also trust colleagues not to ridicule them for half-baked or seemingly silly ideas. The more fear is removed from an organization, the more people will feel free to open up, share ideas, and try new things. Although not all relationships are equal, among teammates who develop a high level of trust there is opportunity for superior collaboration and remarkable outcomes.

continued on next page

Handout 11–19, continued
The Personal Innovation Competencies

Beyond trust, collaborative relationships require respect—for the opinions and concerns of everyone. Some of the best ideas may come from the most unlikely sources throughout the organization. And without the bedrock of relationships that are grounded in honesty, sincere appreciation, and respect for each other's boundaries, serious insights and deep concerns may never come to light.

Some ways to build these competencies:

- Create a "scorecard" for your reliability.
- Make or take time to cultivate relationships with your co-workers.
- Practice listening more attentively.
- Practice expressing appreciation to friends and co-workers.
- Practice expressing your concerns and grounding your assessments.
- Take stock of your relationships and what you give and receive from them.

These are generic ideas—can you think of any more? How can you personalize these ideas?

Category G: Embraces appropriate risk taking

Because innovation, by definition, is doing something that has not been done before, its success is uncertain. Therefore, risk is a requirement of innovation. Many organizations have been risk averse for decades, and now people are being asked to take risks in order to innovate. It's a tricky transition. Organizations that punish people who support the wrong idea will soon find the flow of ideas drying up. Likewise, people who never stick their necks out for new ideas may find their careers will be pale and lackluster.

Knowing the difference between calculated risk and risky business is paramount in innovation. Learning how to advance ideas appropriately can mitigate but not eliminate the risk involved. Many ideas embody risk—some in the mere advancement, others in the execution.

The first step is to understand what the risk represents to stakeholders—is it loss of revenue or profit, is it retribution or the loss of career advancement, is it the danger of bankruptcy? Weighing the risk against potential rewards is the daily work of some financial heads in your organization. In an open environment innovators and their managers can work collaboratively to predict, track, and manage the risks that innovation presents.

Some ways to build these competencies:

- Create a methodology for understanding risks to stakeholders.
- Study the risk/reward models that are used in your industry and elsewhere.
- Interview other innovators about their experiences managing risk.

continued on next page

Handout 11–19, continued

The Personal Innovation Competencies

- Create a communication plan to address risk with stakeholders.
- Find out top management's view on risk taking for innovation.

These are generic ideas—can you think of any more? How can you personalize these ideas?

Category H: Effectively manages innovation projects

Projects must often adjust over time with the changing business and economic climate. By definition, innovation projects should be flexible and follow the value chain. Effective innovators pay close attention to managing promises, juggling priorities, making decisions, and timing for actions. They leverage tools, processes, and methodologies in a conscious fashion to reach intended results.

Most successful organizations are competent in general project management, but the understanding of how to manage an *innovation* project is not always as clear. Innovation project managers must be excellent collaborators, facilitators, and synthesizers. They manage projects and the innovation *process* and help build relationships among team members. They pay attention to timing through continual scanning of the business climate and understanding of the big picture and the concerns of stakeholders.

Master innovators develop criteria in advance and make decisions in a disciplined manner. They establish metrics, track progress, and maintain timely communication with all of the people concerned, adjusting course and actions as needed. When the end is recognized, they celebrate completion, regardless of the project's outcome.

Some ways to build these competencies:

- Get training in project management.
- Determine the differences between routine projects and innovation projects.
- Create a decision-making model.
- Create an inventory of tools, processes, and methodologies around innovation.
- Generate ideas on celebrating both success and failure.

These are generic ideas—can you think of any more? How can you personalize these ideas?

Category I: Learns relentlessly

Master innovators are curious—their endless search for what, how, and why fuels new ideas and vast possibilities. Successful innovation often requires much experimentation and leaves many failures in its wake. Innovators who seek feedback, examine the reasons behind success or failure, and challenge their own assumptions will find themselves constantly propelled forward.

continued on next page

Handout 11-19, continued
The Personal Innovation Competencies

Learning is an itch that is scratched by new information and new understanding. Feeding our curiosity creates a constant flow of new information that stimulates new patterns and understandings. Posing stimulating questions is a common trait of people who become experts at innovation.

Innovation projects can yield enormous knowledge for the organization if lessons are captured and shared widely—whether the project was deemed a success or a failure. Creating a forum for learning, asking questions, and giving and getting feedback is one vehicle for gaining organizational wisdom.

Breaking out of our own world view to accept other perspectives requires that we continually acknowledge and challenge our own assumptions and the assumptions of the organization. It is this constant search for data, insight, and meaning that keeps innovators on the leading edge.

Here are some ways to build these competencies:

- Create a daily practice to help yourself be curious and ask questions.
- Develop a format to conduct "post mortems" on projects to glean lessons learned.
- Create lists of questions that are applicable in recurring situations.
- Determine the assumptions under which you operate and begin questioning them.
- Search for people who are likely to have world views that are very different from yours.

These are generic ideas—can you think of any more? How can you personalize these ideas?

Using the Compact Disc

Insert the CD and locate the file *How to Use This CD.doc.*

Contents of the CD

The compact disc that accompanies this workbook on innovation training contains three types of files. All of the files can be used on a variety of computer platforms.

- **Adobe .pdf documents.** These include figures, handouts, tools, and training instruments.

- **Microsoft PowerPoint presentations.** These presentations add interest and depth to many of the training activities included in the workbook.

- **Microsoft PowerPoint files of overhead transparency masters.** These files makes it easy to print viewgraphs and handouts in black-and-white rather than using an office copier. They contain only text and line drawings; there are no images to print in grayscale.

Computer Requirements

To read or print the .pdf files on the CD, you must have Adobe Acrobat Reader software installed on your system. The program can be downloaded free of cost from the Adobe Website, *www.adobe.com.*

To use or adapt the contents of the PowerPoint presentation files on the CD, you must have Microsoft PowerPoint software installed on your system. If you simply want to view the PowerPoint documents, you must have an appropriate viewer installed on your system. Microsoft provides various viewers free for downloading from its Website, *www.microsoft.com.*

Printing from the CD

TEXT FILES

You can print the training materials using Adobe Acrobat Reader. Simply open the .pdf file and print as many copies as you need. The following .pdf documents can be directly printed from the CD:

- Figure 2–1: InnovationDNA

- Figure 2–2: InnovationDNA (color version)

- Figure 6–1: InnovationDNA Overview Workshop Map

- Figure 6–2: InnovationDNA Overview Workshop Map (color version)

- Figure 7–1: Innovation Comes Alive! Workshop Map

- Figure 7–2: Innovation Comes Alive! Workshop Map (color version)

- Figure 8–1: Creativity Made Simple Workshop Map

- Figure 8–2: Creativity Made Simple Workshop Map (color version)

- Figure 9–1: Personal Innovation Competencies Workshop Map

- Figure 9–2: Personal Innovation Competencies Workshop Map (color version)

- Handout 11–1: What's Your Thinking Style?

- Handout 11–2: Metaphorical Thinking

- Handout 11–3: Springboard Stories

- Handout 11–4: Cracking Questions

- Handout 11–5: Breakthrough Generator Matrix

- Handout 11–6: Better Brainstorming Guidelines

- Handout 11–7: BrainwritingPlus: Powerful and Easy!

- Handout 11–8: Think 360

- Handout 11–9: Quadrant Collaboration

- Handout 11–10: Improving Innovation Ideas

- Handout 11–11: Innovation Criteria Grid

- Handout 11–12: Contemplation Matrix

- Handout 11–13: Creativity Made Simple: SWAMI SOARS!

- Handout 11–14: Dot Voting with a Difference

- Handout 11–15: Dimensions of the InnovationDNA Model

- Handout 11–16: PIC Gap Analysis

- Handout 11–17: PIC Personal Action Worksheet

- Handout 11–18: PIC Discussion Guide

- Handout 11–19: The Personal Innovation Competencies

- Innovation Basics Training Workbook Evaluation Form

- Tool 6–1: InnovationDNA Overview Suggested PowerPoint Script

- Tool 6–2: Innovation Mini-Audit Exercise

- Tool 8–1: Quadrant Chart Example

- Tool 10–1: Quadrant Chart Example

- Training Instrument 3–1: Innovation Mini-Audit

- Training Instrument 5–1: Innovation Training Initial Course Evaluation

- Training Instrument 5–2: Innovation Training Bounce-Back Questionnaire

- Training Instrument 5–3: Sample Notice of Completion with Instructions for Use

- Training Instrument 5–4: Innovation Training Certificate of Completion

POWERPOINT SLIDES

You can print the presentation slides directly from this CD using Microsoft PowerPoint. Simply open the .ppt files and print as many copies as you need.

You can also make handouts of the presentations by printing 2, 4, or 6 "slides" per page. These slides will be in color, with design elements embedded. PowerPoint also permits you to print these in grayscale or black-and-white, although printing from the overhead masters file will yield better black-and-white representations. Many trainers who use personal computers to project their presentations bring along viewgraphs just in case there are glitches in the system.

Adapting the PowerPoint Slides

You can modify or otherwise customize the slides by opening and editing them in the appropriate application. However, you must retain the denotation of the original source of the material—it is illegal to pass it off as your own work. You may indicate that a document was adapted from this workbook, written by Ruth Ann Hattori and Joyce Wycoff and copyrighted by ASTD. The files will open as "Read Only," so before you adapt them you will need to save them onto your hard drive under a different filename.

Showing the PowerPoint Presentations

On the CD, the following PowerPoint presentations are included:

- InnovationDNA.ppt

- Metaphorical Thinking.ppt

- Springboard Stories.ppt

Having the presentations in .ppt format means that it automatically shows full-screen when you double-click on its filename. You also can open Microsoft PowerPoint and launch it from there.

Use the space bar, the enter key, or mouse clicks to advance through a show. Press the backspace key to back up. Use the escape key to abort a presentation. If you want to blank the screen to black while the group discusses a point, press the B key. Pressing it again restores the show. If you want to blank the screen to a white background, do the same with the W key. Table A–1 summarizes these instructions.

We strongly recommend that trainers practice making presentations before using them in training situations. You should be confident that you can cogently expand on the points featured in the presentations and discuss the

Table A-1
Navigating Through a PowerPoint Presentation

KEY	POWERPOINT "SHOW" ACTION
Space bar *or* Enter *or* Mouse click	Advance through custom animations embedded in the presentation
Backspace	Back up to the last projected element of the presentation
Escape	Abort the presentation
B *or* b	Blank the screen to black
B *or* b *(repeat)*	Resume the presentation
W *or* w	Blank the screen to white
W *or* w *(repeat)*	Resume the presentation

methods for working through them. If you want to engage your training participants fully (rather than worrying about how to show the next slide), become familiar with this simple technology *before* you need to use it. A good practice is to insert notes into the *Speaker's Notes* feature of the PowerPoint program, print them out, and have them in front of you when you present the slides.

♦

For Further Reading

BOOKS

There are hundreds of books available in this field. This list is just to give you some of the best to get you started.

Creativity

Ayan, Jordan. *Aha! 10 Ways to Free Your Creative Spirit and Find Your Great Ideas.* New York: Three Rivers Press, 1996.

Cameron, Julia. *The Artist's Way: A Spiritual Path to Higher Creativity.* New York: Jeremy P. Tarcher, 1992.

De Bono, Edward. *Lateral Thinking : Creativity Step by Step.* Perennial, 1973.

Denning, Stephen. *The Springboard: How Storytelling Ignites Action in Knowledge-Era Organizations.* Philadelphia: Elsevier/Butterworth-Heinemann, 2000.

Higgins, James M. *101 Creative Problem Solving Techniques, The Handbook of New Ideas for Business.* New Management Publishing, 1994.

MacKenzie, Gordon. *Orbiting the Giant Hairball: A Corporate Fool's Guide to Surviving with Grace.* New York: Viking Press, 1998.

Michalko, Michael. *Cracking Creativity: The Secrets of Creative Genius.* Berkeley, CA: Ten Speed Press, 1998.

Ray, Michael, and Rochelle Myers. *Creativity in Business.* Mainstream Books, 1998.

Thompson, Charles "Chic." *What a Great Idea! Key Steps Creative People Take.* Perennial, 1992.

von Oech, Roger. *A Whack on the Side of the Head: How You Can Be More Creative.* New York: Warner Business, 1998.

Wolff, Jurgen. *Do Something Different: Proven Marketing Techniques to Transform Your Business.* London: Virgin Publishing, 2001.

Wycoff, Joyce. *Mindmapping, Your Personal Guide to Exploring Creativity and Problem Solving.* Berkeley, CA: Berkley Publishing, 1991.

Innovation

Christensen, Clayton M., and Michael E. Raymor. *The Innovator's Solution: Creating and Sustaining Successful Growth.* Cambridge, MA: Harvard Business School Press, 2003.

Collins, James, and Jerry Porras. *Built to Last.* New York: HarperBusiness, 1997.

Drucker, Peter F. *Innovation and Entrepreneurship: Practice and Principles.* New York: HarperBusiness, 1993.

Dundon, Elaine. *The Seeds of Innovation: Cultivating the Synergy That Fosters New Ideas.* New York: AMACOM, 2002.

Hamel, Gary. *Leading the Revolution.* Cambridge, MA: Harvard Business School Press, 2000.

Kelley, Tom. *The Art of Innovation: Lessons in Creativity from IDEO, America's Leading Design Firm.* Currency, 2001.

Prather, Charles W., and Lisa K. Gundry. *Blueprints for Innovation: How Creative Processes Can Make You and Your Company More Competitive (MA Management Briefing).* New York: AMACOM, 1995.

Rodin, Robert L., and Chris Hartman. *Free, Perfect, and Now.* New York: Simon & Schuster, 1999.

Stack, Jack. *The Great Game of Business.* Currency, 1994.

Tucker, Robert. *Driving Growth through Innovation.* San Francisco: Berrett-Kohler, 2002.

Important Thought Stimulators

Enriquez, Juan. *As the Future Catches You: How Genomics & Other Forces Are Changing Your Life, Work, Health & Wealth.* New York: Crown Business, 2001.

Gladwell, Malcolm. *The Tipping Point: How Little Things Can Make a Big Difference.* New York: Little, Brown, 2000.

Gilmore, James H., and B. Joseph Pine II. *The Experience Economy,* Cambridge, MA: Harvard Business School Press, 1999.

Handy, Charles. *The Hungry Spirit.* New York: Broadway, 1999.

Hock, Dee W. *Birth of the Chaordic Age.* San Francisco: Berrett-Kohler, 2000.

Kohn, Alfie. *Punished by Rewards: The Trouble with Gold Stars, Incentive Plans, A's, Praise, and Other Bribes.* New York: Houghton-Mifflin, 1999.

WEBSITES

American Society for Training & Development, http://astd.org

Fast Company Magazine, http://www.fastcompany.com

Imaginatik Research, http://imaginatik.com

InnovationNetwork, http://thinksmart.com

Innovation Tools, http://innovationtools.com

Product Development Management Association, http://www.pdma.org

Thank you for taking the time to complete this evaluation. Your feedback will help us improve future editions of this workbook. Please respond to each of the statements below by circling the number that corresponds to the following scale:

1 = TOTALLY DISAGREE
2 = MOSTLY DISAGREE
3 = GENERALLY AGREE

4 = MOSTLY AGREE
5 = TOTALLY AGREE

EVALUATION STATEMENT   **RATING**

1.	The workbook objectives were clearly explained.	1 2 3 4 5
2.	The workbook objectives were achieved.	1 2 3 4 5
3.	The workbook met my expectations.	1 2 3 4 5
4.	Good learning principles and processes were used.	1 2 3 4 5
5.	I learned new ideas or tools that are applicable to my job.	1 2 3 4 5
6.	The learning activities were engaging and well presented.	1 2 3 4 5
7.	The handouts were easy to use and inviting.	1 2 3 4 5
8.	The workbook presented a coherent and useable program.	1 2 3 4 5
9.	I now feel comfortable offering innovation training.	1 2 3 4 5

10. What was most useful to you about this book?

11. Have you presented workshops shown in this book? If so, what type of modifications to them did you make?

12. What suggestions for improvement do you have?

Name (optional):_____ Email address: _____

Please fax this evaluation form to 775-593-4187 or fill out the form on the CD and email it to jwycoff@thinksmart.com.

As co-founder of InnovationNetwork®, **Ruth Ann Hattori** has studied how innovation occurs in countless organizations. She has created dozens of learning experiences for individuals and organizations on the topic of innovation, including the annual innovation conference, Convergence.

Having enjoyed remarkable success in the apparel industry for 20 years, Hattori brings a pragmatic business perspective to her work in both innovation and organizational effectiveness. After leaving her post as president of Rocky Mountain Clothing Co., she joined InnovationNetwork, during its transition from a professional association to a business education and virtual innovation resource center. She has led their InnovationUniversity™ program, written articles on innovation, and created innovation assessment tools.

In addition to her research and writing with InnovationNetwork, Hattori is a principal of Customer Contact Corporation (C^3), working directly with organizations to help them improve their collaborative and innovative practices.

A founding fellow of InnovationUniversity and alumnus of the Creative Problem Solving Institute, Hattori is passionate about the people side of innovation. She has studied continuous improvement, behavioral linguistics, accelerated learning, and numerous art and creative techniques for learning, and has found a way to bring all of those elements together in a manner that helps organizations be more effective.

Joyce Wycoff is the co-founder of the InnovationNetwork®. For the past 11 years she has studied and articulated the system of innovation and created ways to share findings with innovation practitioners around the world. Since 1994 she has brought leading innovation thinkers and practitioners to a gathering known as Convergence so that they can share their ideas, experiences, and great practices.

Wycoff is a popular keynote speaker, trainer, and facilitator as well as the author of four personal productivity books focused on creativity and innovation. Two of these books (*Mindmapping* and *To Do, Doing, Done!*) have achieved best-selling classic status and have been published in several languages. She writes a weekly electronic column for some 15,000 readers and has written numerous magazine articles, booklets, and video scripts.

Wycoff is a die-hard optimist who believes in the proverbial "better way." Life has also taught her to be a pragmatist—to look for better ways that "work." Her professional background has been a journey from financial management to creativity and innovation, with a lot of side trips along the way. She fervently believes that a committed group of people can change an organization and that enough changed organizations can create a better world.

Wycoff fervently encourages people to explore their personal creativity, and her own creative journey focuses on poetry and intuitive painting. She includes poetry, collage, metaphorical thinking, and other creative exercises in all of her business workshops and keynote speeches.